THE LOUISIANA PROUD COLLECTION OF SWEET THINGS

LOUISIANA PROUD ©

Compiled by
Andy Smith and Kirby Ward

Illustrated by
Andy Smith

Edited by
Evelyn Duke

A LOUISIANA PROUD PRESS BOOK

For Information Contact
Louisiana Proud
6133 Goodwood Ave.
Baton Rouge, Louisiana 70806

Other Louisiana Proud Press Publications:
Louisiana Proud Volume I
Louisiana Proud Volume II
Louisiana Proud Volume III
Rouxdolph's Gumbo and Soup Book
The Louisiana Proud Collection of Home Cooking

Dedicated to all Louisiana cooks and especially to the Louisianians who made this book a reality by sharing one of their recipes with us.

SPECIAL THANKS

Jane P. Ogea

Like the Louisiana Proud Collection of Home Cooking, this book would not have been completed without the overall efforts of Jane.   She typeset virtually all the recipes and shared the proofing with Mrs. Duke. She also helped with page composition. Probably most important, she kept everything running smoothly and organized.

Mrs. Evelyn Duke

Inspiring and guiding the concept of the Louisiana Proud Collection of Home Cooking, Mrs. Duke took on the duties of editing this Collection. A long time resident of Columbia and a retired home economist in Caldwell Parish, Mrs. Duke has blended her experience from the classroom to the kitchen in the editing of this book. She also acquired some of her fellow home economists and friends favorite recipes.

THE LOUISIANA PROUD COLLECTION

The Louisiana Proud Collection is a collection of photo-graphs and pen and ink illustrations of the buildings of the State. All the illustrations in this book are taken from the collection. The collection was started in 1982. It now con-tains over 1700 illustrations and 18,000 photographs. This ongoing project focuses on the everyday buildings of Louisi-ana. From this collection, three hardbound volumns of the histories of the towns were produced. The Collection is an attempt to record what the State really looks like.

In order to obtain these photographs the entire State was crisscrossed many times. One part of the discovery of the State is observing the different faces of the landscape. Another was the sampling of the different tastes of the State. This second reason was the inspiration for the Loui-siana Proud Collection of Home Cooking.

In order to complete the Cooking Collection, The Louisiana Proud Collection of Sweet Things was put together.

HOW RECIPES WERE OBTAINED

A form was prepared with the title "The Louisiana Proud Collection of Home Cooking is not finished. It is now time for the dessert!" As with the first book, each town was visited and a person who lived there was asked to give us a recipe. It should be something that they prepare for their families, one of their favorites. Pies, Cakes, Cookies, Candies, Puddings, Jellies or anything sweet was the only requirement.

The Louisiana Proud Collection of Sweet Things is taken from the entire State. Each recipe comes from a person who lives and works in the town. Each recipe is illustrated with a building from that town. The book is intended to give you the taste and look of Louisiana.

TABLE OF CONTENTS

HOW THE BOOK IS DIVIDED
A note about the layout of the book will make it easier to
find a specific town. As in the Louisiana Proud Book Series,
the Cookbook is broken into 5 sections. These sections
relate to the geographical sections of the State, (Southeast,
Southwest, etc.)

The Table of Contents will bring you to the start of each
section. There you will find an alphabetical listing of each
town represented and a map of the section you are about to
enter. The towns are in alphabetical order until you reach
the next section.

There are also indexes by town and by recipe category in
the back of the book.

Southeast Section

Abita Springs
Addis
Albany
Ama
Amite
Angie
Baker
Baton Rouge
Bogalusa
Bourg
Brusly
Buras
Central
Chalmette
Clinton
Convent
Covington
Cut Off
Denham Springs
Destrahan
Donaldsonville
Dulac
Dutchtown
Edgard
Erwinville
Ethel

Folsom
Franklinton
French Settlement
Galliano
Garyville
Geismar
Golden Meadow
Gonzales
Gramercy
Grand Isle
Greensburg
Gretna
Grosse Tete
Hahnville
Hammond
Harahan
Hardwood
Houma
Independence
Innis
Jackson
Kenner
Kentwood
Labadieville
Laplace

Livingston
Livonia
Lockport
Luling
Lutcher
Madisonville
Mandeville
Maringouin
Maurepas
Metairie
Montpelier
Morganza
Napoleonville
New Orleans
New Roads
Norco
Norwood
Pierre Part
Pine Grove
Plaquemine
Ponchatoula
Port Allen
Port Sulphur
Port Vincent
Prairieville

Raceland   Springfield   Violet
Reiley   St. Bernard   Walker
Reserve   St. Francisville White Castle
Rosedale   Thibodaux   Whitehall
Slaughter   Tickfaw   Zachary
Slidell   Vacherie
Sorrento   Varnado

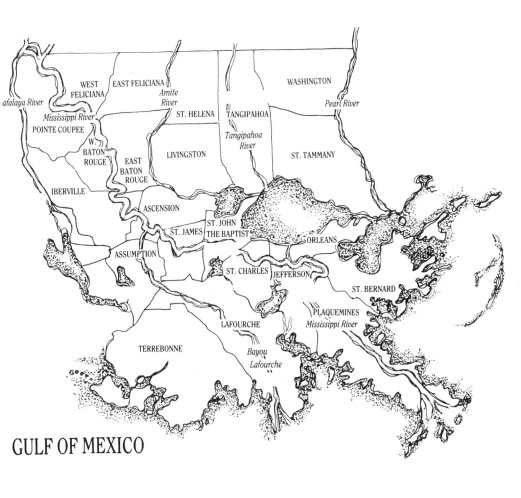

GULF OF MEXICO

Blackberry Surprise

SERVES 8-10

1 box plain yellow cake mix
2 cups blackberries
1/4 cup sugar
SAUCE:
2 eggs
2 tbsp. sugar
1/4 tsp. salt
1 quart milk
2/3 cup sugar
1/2 tsp. vanilla
1/4 tsp. nutmeg

Prepare cake mix as directed. Wash blackberries, sprinkle with sugar, lightly fold blackberries into cake batter and bake in layer pan as directed. Separate eggs and beat whites until they are foamy. Gradually add sugar and beat until stiff. Cream egg yokes with sugar, salt and vanilla. Scald milk and add gradually to egg mixture, mixing well. Lightly fold in egg whites. Add nutmeg. Chill sauce and serve over blackberry cake. Enjoy!

ABITA SPRINGS

Sue Wolfe
ST. TAMMANY PARISH

Missy's Pudding Cookies

MAKES 6 DOZEN

2 1/4 cups flour
1 tsp. baking soda
1 cup butter
1/4 cup sugar
3/4 cup light brown sugar
1 small pack vanilla instant pudding
1 tsp. vanilla
2 eggs
1 (12 oz.) package milk chocolate chips
1 cup pecans

Mix flour and baking soda and set aside. Cream butter, sugars and pudding until smooth. Add eggs and vanilla, beat well. Add flour and baking soda and mix well. Add chocolate chips and pecans. Drop teaspoon size dough on ungreased cookie sheet and bake at 375 degrees for 8 to 10 minutes.

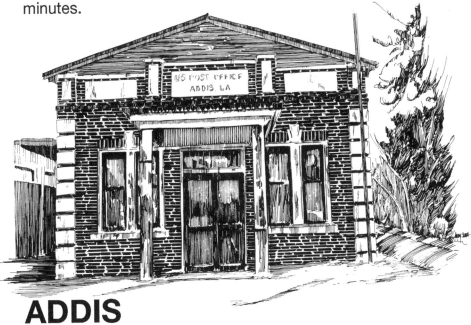

ADDIS

Zella V. Blanchard
WEST BATON ROUGE PARISH

Extra Moist Brownies

SERVES 6

1 stick margarine, softened
3/4 cup flour
3/4 cup white sugar
3/4 cup brown sugar
1 tsp. baking powder
4 tbsp. cocoa powder
2 eggs
2 tsp. vanilla

Blend together margarine and sugar. Add eggs, one at a time. Sift flour, cocoa and baking powder. Add to above mixture. Add vanilla. Pour into a greased 9" X 9" pan. Bake in 350 degree oven for 30 minutes. Will be soft until cooled.

ALBANY

Dorothy Kropog
LIVINGSTON PARISH

Peanut Butter Fudge

SERVES 50

1 stick butter
6 cups sugar
3 cups milk
2 tsp. vanilla
Dash of salt
1/2 cup peanut butter
1 1/3 cups cocoa

Mix sugar and cocoa together, put in dash of salt and pour in milk. Stir until sugar is dissolved. Turn stove on medium to high heat. You must stir mixture until fudge starts to boil. When fudge starts to boil put stove on medium and let it boil slowly until mixture thickens. When mixture thickens, test by putting a small amount of mixture into a glass of cool water. If mixture forms a ball, turn fire off. Let mixture stand for 5 to 10 minutes or the time it takes to butter your cookie sheet. Put 1 stick of butter into mixture along with peanut butter and vanilla. Stir until mixture looses is glossy look or mixture starts to get hard. Pour onto cookie sheet. This recipe is a double batch and will yield about 125 pieces of fudge, that is about an inch square. Cut fudge while warm and firm.

AMA

Joyce P. Horn
ST. CHARLES PARISH

Chocolate Cake

SERVES 10-12

2/3 cup soft shortening
1 1/2 cups sugar
3 eggs
2 1/2 squares unsweetened chocolate, melted
2 1/4 cups sifted Softasilk flour
1 tsp. soda
1 tsp. salt
1 1/4 cups buttermilk

Grease and flour 2 round baking pans. Cream together until fluffy, the sugar and eggs. Beat 5 minutes on high speed. Blend in chocolate. Sift together flour, soda and salt. Mix in alternately the flour and buttermilk. Pour into prepared pans. Bake at 350 degrees for 30 to 35 minutes. Frost with chocolate butter icing.

AMITE

R. E. Goldsby M.D., Mayor of Amite
TANGIPAHOA PARISH

Strawberry Chiffon Pie

SERVES 6

1 pt. strawberries, fresh
1/2 cup sugar
1 box strawberry Jello
2/3 cup cold water
1 tbsp. lemon juice
2 egg whites
1/4 cup sugar
1/2 cup whipping cream
1 (9") baked pie shell
Dash of salt

Crush strawberries with 1/2 cup sugar and let stand for 30 minutes. Soften gelatin in water, dissolve over low heat and cool. Add strawberries, lemon juice and dash of salt. Chill, stirring occasionally until partially set. Beat egg whites and gradually add 1/4 cup sugar and beat until stiff peaks form. Fold into strawberry mixture. Add whipped cream and chill until mixture mounds. Pile into cooled pie shell. Chill until firm.

ANGIE

Hilda Breland
WASHINGTON PARISH

Ding Dong Cake

SERVES 10-12

1 box devil's food cake mix
4 tbsp. flour
1 cup milk
1/2 cup butter or margarine
1 cup sugar
1/2 cup shortening
1 tsp. vanilla
Pinch of salt

FROSTING:
1 stick margarine
4 tbsp. cocoa
6 tbsp. milk
1 tsp. vanilla
1 (1lb.) box powdered sugar

Mix and bake cake according to package directions, using 9" X 13" pan instructions. Cool cake and split in half horizontally. Blend milk into flour. Cook over medium heat, stirring constantly until thickened. Cool completely. Beat margarine or butter, shortening and sugar 4 minutes with electric mixer. Add to cooled flour mixture. Beat 4 minutes, add vanilla and salt. Whip with mixer until fluffy. Spread over one of the cut cake halves. Then top with the other cake half. FROSTING: Mix margarine, cocoa and milk. Bring to a boil. Remove from heat. Add sugar and vanilla. Beat until mixture reaches a spreading consistency.

BAKER

Phyllis Bryant
EAST BATON ROUGE PARISH

Apple Pie

SERVES 8

2 uncooked pie shells
5-6 tart apples, peeled and sliced to fill pie shell
2/3 cup sugar
1 tsp. cinnamon
1 tsp. corn starch
1 tbsp. butter
1 tbsp. lemon juice

Mix sugar, cinnamon and corn starch. Sprinkle this mixture over apples in uncooked pie shell. Dot butter over apples. Place second pie shell over apple mixture and seal pie shells by pressing together with fork. Make 4 slats in top of pie shell to allow steam to escape. Bake in 350 degree oven until crust browns, approximately 50-60 minutes.

BATON ROUGE

Annie F. Ward
EAST BATON ROUGE PARISH

Addictive Cookies

MAKES 7 DOZEN

1cup butter
1 cup sugar
1 cup brown sugar
1 egg
1 cup salad oil
1 cup rolled oats
1 cup crushed cornflakes
1/2 cup flaked coconut
1 cup pecan meal
3 1/2 cups flour
1 tsp. soda
1 tsp. salt
1 tsp. vanilla

Preheat oven to 325 degrees. Cream butter and sugars until light and fluffy. Add egg and blend. Add salad oil, stirring until oil is well blended. Add oats, cornflakes, coconut and pecan meal. Stir until mixed. Add flour, soda, salt and vanilla and mix well. Form balls about the size of a walnut. Place on an ungreased cookie sheet and flatten with a fork dipped in water. Bake 12 minutes. Allow to cool for a few minutes before removing.

BOGALUSA

Dr. Lynn Porter Alexander
WASHINGTON PARISH

Blackberry Dumplings

SERVES 10

1/2 gallon blackberries
 or dewberries
Water
2 1/2 cups sugar
1 cup Bisquick
1 cup self-rising flour

2 tbsp. sugar
1/2 cup milk
1 tsp. vanilla
1 egg
1/2 tsp. apple spice
 or cinnamon

Cover blackberries with water and boil for 10 minutes. Press through a sieve. Return juice to pot and add 2 1/2 cups sugar and boil to a thin syrup. While this is boiling, prepare dumplings. In a small mixing bowl, beat egg. Add milk and vanilla. In a large mixing bowl, combine Bisquick, flour, sugar and spice. Pour egg mixture into dry ingredients to form a drop batter. Dip a large tablespoon into water then into batter. Drop by spoonful into hot berry syrup. Use a wide pot. Cook on medium flame until dumplings puff. Roll over once and cover pot. Cook for about 5 minutes. Remove dumplings to large shallow dish. Add more dumplings to syrup and repeat process until all batter is used. If you find syrup too thick, add a little water to syrup and bring to a boil before adding more batter. After all dumplings are cooked, pour the remaining syrup over dumplings. Best served warm.

BOURG

Kathleen B. Barber
TERREBONNE PARISH

Chocolate Chip Cheesecake

SERVES 8

18 finely crushed Oreos
2-3 tbsp. butter, melted
1 can condensed milk
3 eggs
2 tsp. vanilla
1 cup mini semi-sweet chocolate chips
1 tsp. flour
3 (8 oz.) packages cream cheese

Preheat oven to 350 degrees. Combine cookies and butter. Press in the bottom of a springform pan. In a large bowl, beat cheese until fluffy. Gradually beat in milk. Add eggs and vanilla. Mix well. In a small bowl, toss 1/2 cup chips with flour to coat. Stir into cheese mixture. Pour into prepared pan. Sprinkle with remaining chips evenly over top. Bake for 1 hour. Turn oven off and allow cheesecake to cool in oven. Chill for several hours before serving.

BRUSLY

Rose B. Tullier & Ann Marie Hill
WEST BATON ROUGE PARISH

Chocolate Cream Cake

SERVES 24

1 box devil food cake mix (Duncan Hines)
2 small boxes of instant chocolate pudding
1 (16 oz.) Cool Whip or any whip topping
2 (9") baking pans (round or square)

Cake: Mix cake as directed on box, adding 1 box of chocolate pudding. Bake as directed, test with toothpick to see if done. Cool in baking pans for 15 minutes. Put in freezer for at least 2 hours. Remove from baking pans and split each layer with thread/dental floss. Put cardboard between layers and return to freezer. Frosting: In a large bowl put whip topping then sprinkle small box of chocolate pudding over topping and mix well with spatula. Frosting should be creamy. If too thick, add milk a little at a time until smooth enough to spread on layers. Have cake layer on covered board, spread frosting over each layer until completely covered.

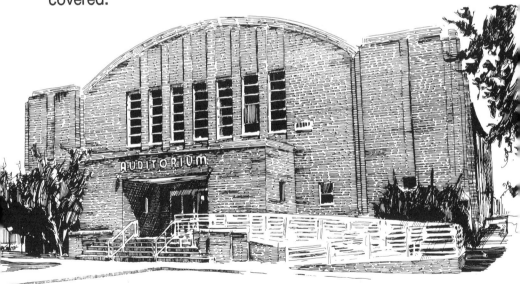

BURAS

Mrs. Judy Petkovich
PLAQUEMINES PARISH

Fresh Apple Cake

SERVES 12

1 cup cooking oil
2 cups sugar
3 eggs, beaten
2 1/2 cups all-purpose flour
2 tsp. baking powder
1 tsp. baking soda
1 tsp. salt
1 tsp. nutmeg
1 tsp. vanilla
4 cups apples,diced and pared
1 cup pecans, chopped
1 tsp. cinnamon

ICING:
1 box confectioners sugar
1/2 cup butter
1 cup chopped pecans
1 (8 oz.) package
   Philadelphia cream cheese
2 tsp. vanilla

Combine oil and sugar. Beat in eggs. Sift dry ingredients together an add to egg mixture. Fold in vanilla, apples and pecans. Bake in 13" X 9" pan for 55 minutes at 325 degrees. Cool and ice with vanilla cream cheese icing. ICING: Beat sugar and cream cheese until soft and smooth. Add vanilla and pecans. Ice cooled cake in pan. To serve, cut into squares.

CENTRAL

Olive H. Randall
EAST BATON ROUGE PARISH

Russian Cookies

SERVES 15-20

3 eggs
3 cups flour, plain
2 sticks butter
1 cup raisins
2 cups pecans, chopped
3/4 cup sugar
2 tsp. cinnamon
1 tsp. vanilla
1 box chopped dates
1 tsp. baking soda
1 tbsp. hot water

Cream butter, add sugar, then beat eggs and mix with above. Add 3 cups flour. Mix raisins, pecans and dates. Mix soda and water together and add to above. Add vanilla and cinnamon. Make small balls, place on greased cookie sheet and place in 350 degree oven until brown.

CHALMETTE

Ruth B. Zulli
ST. BERNARD PARISH

23

Chocolate Pecan Chess Pie

SERVES 6

1 stick butter or oleo, melted
1 cup sugar
2 eggs
1/2 cup flour
1 tsp. vanilla
1 cup pecans, chopped
1 (6 oz.) package chocolate chips
1 (9") unbaked pie shell

Cream butter and sugar. Add eggs, one at a time, beat well. Stir in flour, vanilla and pecans and mix well. Fill bottom of pie shell with chocolate chips then add filling. Bake at 350 degrees for 40-50 minutes. Best served warm.

CLINTON

Evelyn P. Beauchamp
EAST FELICIANA PARISH

Pecan Pralines

SERVES 10-12

2 cups sugar
2 cups pecan halves
1 large can evaporated milk

Boil slowly the sugar and milk. Just before reaching the soft ball stage, add the pecans. This gives the pecans a toasted taste. When the soft ball stage is reached, remove from the heat and let cool and then beat until creamy. Drop the mixture by spoonfuls on waxed paper; they are real easy to remove.

CONVENT

Ethel M. Roussel
ST. JAMES PARISH

Ed's Grape Ice Cream

SERVES 10

2 1/2 cups grape juice
5 lemons, juice only
2 pints Half and Half
1/2 pint whipping cream
1/2 pint milk
2 cups sugar

Mix all ingredients. Turn in ice cream mixer until done. The color is a beautiful lavender ice cream. Delicious and very smooth.

COVINGTON

Edward Greenwald
ST. TAMMANY PARISH

Apple Crunch

SERVES 8-12

2 cans apple pie filling
3/4 cup brown sugar
1 1/2 tsp. cinnamon
1 box yellow cake mix
1 box vanilla instant pudding
1 cup chopped pecans
2 sticks melted butter

Cover the bottom of a 13" X 9" X 2" pan with pie filling.
Layer brown sugar, cinnamon, dry cake mix and dry vanilla
instant pudding, one at a time in order of sequence.
Sprinkle pecans on top. Now cover with melted butter.
Bake at 350 degrees for 45 minutes or until golden brown.

CUT OFF

Michelle D. Guilbeaux
LAFOURCHE PARISH

Sinful Blueberry Delight

SERVES 12

1 angel food cake
3 pt. blueberries
1/3 cup sugar
2 cans condensed milk
1 large container Cool Whip
1 (11 oz.) package cream cheese

Combine blueberries and sugar. Cook 10 minutes then cool. Break angel food cake into small pieces. Put pieces into a 11" X 14" pan. Mix condensed milk, Cool Whip and cream cheese and pour over cake. Top with blueberries. Refrigerate.

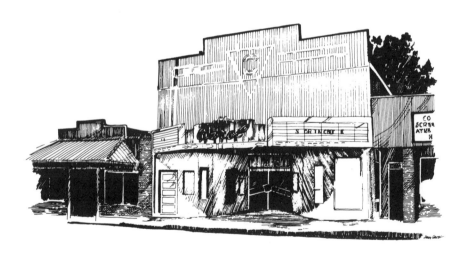

DENHAM SPRINGS

Jane Rousseau
LIVINGSTON PARISH

Turtle Cake

SERVES 16-20

1 box German chocolate cake mix
1 (14 oz.) bag Kraft caramels
1/2 cup Pet milk
3/4 cup butter
2 cups pecans
2 cups chocolate chips

Prepare cake mix according to package directions. Pour
1/2 of the cake batter in a greased and floured 9" X 13"
cake pan. Bake 15 minutes at 350 degrees. In a saucepan,
melt the caramels, milk and butter, stirring constantly. Pour
over cake. Sprinkle 1 cup pecans and 1 cup chocolate
chips. Pour the rest of the batter. Sprinkle remaining
pecans and chips. Bake for 20 more minutes. Do not
overbake.

DESTRAHAN

Hollie Louque Ericksen
ST. CHARLES PARISH

Lemon Delight

SERVES 10

1/2 cup pecans
1 cup self-rising flour
1/2 cup soft butter
1 (12 oz.) box cream cheese
1 cup Cool Whip
1 cup confectioners sugar
2 packages instant lemon pudding
3 cups milk

Mix first three ingredients together and press into the bottom of a 9" X 12 " baking pan or Pyrex dish. Bake at 350 degrees for 20 minutes or until light brown. Cool. Mix next three ingredients together and pour on top of crust. Mix last two ingredients and pour on top of cream cheese mixture. Top with Cool Whip if desired. Chill before serving.

DONALDSONVILLE

Ann H. Dill
ASCENSION PARISH

Nin's Strawberry Chocolate Delight

SERVES 10-12

1 box Duncan Hines butter recipe fudge cake mix
3 eggs
1/2 cup margarine
3/4 cup water
2 small boxes Jello instant chocolate fudge pudding & pie filling
4 cups cold milk
1 can strawberry pie filling or
2 cups fresh sliced strawberries
1 pack strawberry glaze
1 large container Cool Whip

Prepare cake mix as per instructions on box. Let cool and then cut into 2" by 2" squares. Prepare Jello pudding as per instructions on box. Refrigerate until you are ready to put the cake together. If you are using fresh strawberries instead of the ready made pie filling, mix the fresh strawberries with the strawberry glaze. In a bowl 10" in diameter and at least 4 1/2" high, place one layer of cake across the bottom of the bowl. Spoon a layer of pudding on top of cake. Spread half of the container of Cool Whip on top of pudding. Spread half of the strawberry mixture on top of Cool Whip. Repeat layers ending with Cool Whip.

DULAC

Nirmala Hebert Voisin
TERREBONNE PARISH

31

Million Dollar Pie

SERVES 10

1 can condensed milk
Juice of 2 lemons
1 can peaches, cut up and drained
1 can crushed pineapple, drained
1/2 cup coconut
1/2 cup chopped pecans
3 doz. cherries
1 large container Cool Whip
2 graham cracker pie shells

Mix lemon juice with condensed milk. Add peaches, pine-apple, coconut, cherries and pecans to mixture. Add Cool Whip and mix well. Pour into pie shells. Refrigerate or may be frozen.

DUTCHTOWN

Mrs. Gloria Long
ASCENSION PARISH

Betty Boo's Creole Bread Pudding

SERVES 20

1 large French bread
1 small French bread
1/2 gallon milk
2 cans evaporated milk
2 cups sugar
6 eggs
3 blocks butter, softened
1 large can crushed pineapple
1/2 jar cherries, cut in pieces
2 tsp. cherry juice
1 cup raisins

1 tsp. each:
  vanilla
  butternut extract
  almond extract
  pineapple extract
  banana extract
  lemon extract
SAUCE:
2 blocks butter
2 cups sugar
2 eggs
1/4 cup rum or whiskey

Use a pan that is approximately 10" X 15" X 3". Set oven to 350 degrees. Cut French bread in 1/2" slices. Put in pan and pour evaporated milk and almost all of the 1/2 gallon of milk over bread to soak. Set aside. Cream softened butter. Add sugar, a little at a time. Add eggs, one at a time. Beat until creamy. Add flavorings and beat well. Add cherries, pineapples, raisins and cherry juice to bread. Add butter mixture to bread and mix well. Place in preheated oven for about one hour or until firm. Remove from heat and add whiskey or rum sauce. SAUCE: In saucepan, caramelize butter and sugar until thick and creamy. Beat eggs and add to butter mixture. Beat quickly so eggs don't curdle. Remove from heat and add liquor. Pour over bread pudding.

EDGARD

Betty P. Tassin

ST. JOHN THE BAPTIST PARISH

Fig Cake

SERVES 10

2 cups sugar
1 cup cooking oil
3 large eggs
1 cup figs
2 cups flour
1 tsp. soda
1 tsp. allspice
1 tsp. cinnamon
1 tsp. nutmeg
1 tsp. cloves
1/2 tsp. salt
2/3 cup buttermilk
2 cups chopped pecans or raisins

Mix all ingredients together. Cook in greased tube pan at 350 degrees for 1 1/2 hours.

ERWINVILLE

Pamela Neal Lurry
WEST BATON ROUGE PARISH

Granny's Toasted Pecan or Walnut Pralines

MAKES 3 1/2 DOZEN

1 (1 lb.) box light brown sugar
1 small can Pet milk
2 tbsp. white Karo
2 tbsp. water
1/2 stick butter or margarine
3 cups toasted pecans or walnuts

Mix in pot, brown sugar, Pet milk, Karo and water. Bring to a boil stirring occasionally until mixture forms a soft ball when dropped into a cup of cold water. Remove from heat and add butter stirring continually until mixture becomes creamy. Immediately add pecans and drop by teaspoonful onto waxed paper. Pecans or walnuts can be toasted in microwave on microwaveable plate on high for 3 minutes, turn and stir. Microwave for additional 3 to 4 minutes. Be sure to check after the first 3 minutes.

THE OLD STORE

ETHEL

Vera C. Peel
EAST FELICIANA PARISH

Louisiana Nut Cake

SERVES 10

1 cup butter
6 eggs
4 cups flour
1 package raisins
2 qt. pecans
1 tsp. cinnamon
2 cups sugar
1 cup whiskey
1 tsp. allspice
2 packages dates, chopped
1 tsp. soda
1 tsp. cloves

Cream butter and sugar. Add eggs, one at a time, beating after each addition. Dredge nuts, dates and raisins in 2 cups of the flour. Mix remaining flour with spices and soda. Add to butter mixture alternately with whiskey. Fold in nuts, dates and raisins, which have been coated with flour. Bake in greased and floured tube, angel or bundt pan at 250 degrees for about 2 hours. This cake freezes well.

FOLSOM

Sharon Irvin
ST .TAMMANY PARISH

Chocolate Pecan Pie

SERVES 8

3 eggs, slightly beaten
1 cup light corn syrup
4 squares semi-sweet chocolate
1/3 cup sugar
2 tbsp. butter
1 tbsp. vanilla
1 1/2 cups pecan pieces
1 pie shell

Melt and cool the chocolate. Add eggs, syrup, sugar, butter and vanilla until well blended. Add pecans and pour into a partially baked pie shell. Bake about 1 hour in a 350 degree oven or until set. Cool before cutting.

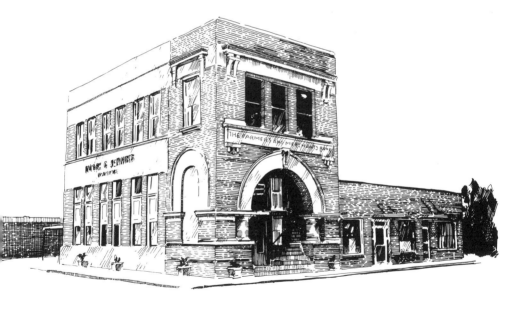

FRANKLINTON

Carole Knight
WASHINGTON PARISH

Spice Cake

SERVES 10-12

3 cups flour
1 cup oil
1 large spoon vanilla
2 cups sugar
3 eggs
Allspice

Mix all ingredients together, pour into greased pan. Bake at 350 degrees for 45 minutes or until done.

FRENCH SETTLEMENT

Judy Baldwin
LIVINGSTON PARISH

Chocolate Eclair Cake

SERVES 12-14

1 box graham crackers
2 small boxes instant pudding,
  French vanilla
3 cups cold milk
1 large Cool Whip

FROSTING:
1 cup sugar
1/3 cup cocoa
1/4 cup milk
1 stick margarine
1 tsp. vanilla

Mix pudding and milk. Add Cool Whip. Butter 13" X 9" baking pan. Layer graham crackers in pan then 1 layer of pudding mixture. Alternate layers ending with graham crackers on top. FROSTING: Bring first 3 ingredients to a boil. Boil for 1 minute. Remove from heat. Add margarine and vanilla. Stir until melted. Pour and spread evenly over graham crackers. Refrigerate overnight.

GALLIANO

Karla Cheramie
LAFOURCHE PARISH

Lemon Fluff

SERVES 8

1 cup flour
1 stick butter
1 cup chopped pecans
1 (8 oz.) package Philadelphia cream cheese
1 (9 oz.) container Cool Whip
1 cup powdered sugar
2 (3 oz.) packages instant lemon pudding

Mix flour, butter and pecans and press down evenly and bake in a 13" X 9" pan at 350 degrees for 15 minutes. Mix cream cheese and sugar and spread carefully on crust. Mix pudding as directed on package except use 3 cups of milk not 4. Spread on cream cheese layer and top with Cool Whip.

GARYVILLE

Gloria Triche/San Francisco Plantation
ST. JOHN THE BAPTIST PARISH

40

Cajun Cake

SERVES 10-12

2 cups all-purpose flour
1 1/2 cups sugar
1 1/2 tsp. soda
Pinch of salt
2 eggs
1 large can crushed pineapple
TOPPING:
1 stick butter or oleo
1 cup sugar
1 tsp. vanilla
1 small can evaporated milk
1 cup chopped pecans
1 cup grated or flaked coconut

Mix together all cake ingredients and beat by hand for 4 minutes. Bake at 300 degrees for 40 minutes in long greased baking dish. TOPPING: Mix oleo, milk and sugar together and boil for 5 minutes. Add vanilla, nuts and coconut and spread on hot cake. Cut in squares and serve.

GEISMAR

Suzanne Geismar George
ASCENSION PARISH

Chocolate Fudge Cake

SERVES 12

2 cups sugar
2 cups flour
1/2 cup Crisco shortening
1 stick oleo or butter
3 tbsp. cocoa powder
1 cup water
1/2 cup buttermilk
1 tsp. baking soda
1 tsp. vanilla
2 eggs

ICING:
1 stick oleo or butter
6 tbsp. Pet milk
3 tbsp. cocoa powder
1 (1lb.) box powdered sugar
1 tsp. vanilla
1-1 1/2cups chopped pecans

Mix sugar and flour, then set aside. In a saucepan bring shortening, butter, cocoa powder and water to a boil. In another bowl mix buttermilk, baking soda, vanilla and eggs together. Now stir together all of the ingredients. Pour mixture in a well greased and floured 13" X 9" X 2" pan. Bake at 350 degrees for 35 minutes. As soon as the cake is done begin preparing the icing. In a saucepan bring butter, Pet milk and cocoa powder to a boil. Remove from stove. Stir in powdered sugar, vanilla and pecans. Spread this warm mixture over cake. Don't let icing cool before spreading on cake because it will harden.

GOLDEN MEADOW

Estelle Callais
LAFOURCHE PARISH

Easy Carrot Cake
SERVES 20

1 box yellow cake mix
1 1/4 cups salad dressing
4 eggs
1/4 cup cold water
2 tsp. cinnamon
2 cups carrots, finely shredded
1/2 cup walnuts, chopped
1 (16 oz.) tub vanilla frosting, optional

Combine in a large bowl; cake mix, salad dressing, eggs, water and cinnamon. Mix with electric mixer at medium speed until well blended. Stir in carrots and walnuts. Pour into a well greased 13" X 9" pan or a bundt pan. Bake at 350 degrees for 45 minutes or until toothpick inserted in center comes out clean. Cool. Frost if desired.

GONZALES

Juanita Andrepont Hunt
ASCENSION PARISH

43

Ooey Gooey Squares

SERVES 15-20

1 package Duncan Hines butter cake mix
1 stick oleo
1 cup chopped pecans
3 eggs
1 (8 oz.) package Philadelphia cream cheese
1 box Colonial powdered sugar

Mix together cake mix, butter and 1 egg. Mix well. Add chopped pecans. Pat into a 13" X 9" X 2" ungreased pan. Cream together the cream cheese, 2 eggs and powdered sugar. Pour over crust. Bake at 350 degrees for 45 minutes. Cut into squares when cool.

GRAMERCY

Elwin G. Millet
ST. JAMES PARISH

Black Bottom Pie

SERVES 6-8

1 stick butter
1 cup flour
1/2 cup chopped nuts
1 (8 oz.) package cream cheese
1 (9 oz.) carton Cool Whip
1 cup powdered sugar
1 small package vanilla instant pudding
1 small package chocolate instant pudding

Cream butter, flour and nuts. Spread in 9" X 13" pan. Bake at 350 degrees until light brown. Cool 15 minutes. Blend together cream cheese, Cool Whip and powdered sugar. Spread on crust. Prepare vanilla and chocolate puddings according to package directions. Pour over cream cheese mixture. Top with Cool Whip and sprinkle with nuts and chill.

GRAND ISLE

Venona E. Bergmann
JEFFERSON PARISH

Blueberry Cobbler

SERVES 8

1 cup self-rising flour
1 cup milk
1 cup sugar
1 cup melted butter
1 cup blueberries

Combine milk, sugar, flour and 3/4 cups of butter. Stir well. Pour into baking dish and pour remainder of butter on top of the mixture. Pour blueberries on top. Place uncovered into oven and bake at 375 degrees for 30 minutes. Serve with vanilla ice cream.

GREENSBURG

MaryJo Cutrer
ST. HELENA PARISH

Peanut Butter Surprise Cookies

MAKES 6 DOZEN

2 1/4 cups all-purpose flour
2 sticks butter or 1 cup margarine
1 tsp. baking soda
1 cup firmly packed brown sugar
1 cup granulated sugar
1 tsp. vanilla
1/2 tsp. salt
2 eggs
1 (6 oz.) bag chocolate morsels
3 tbsp. peanut butter

Mix flour, salt and baking soda and set aside. Mix melted margarine, brown sugar, granulated sugar, vanilla, eggs and peanut butter. Mix well. Blend above ingredients together. Add chocolate morsels. Mix well. Spoon onto cookie sheet by teaspoon. Bake in a 350 degree oven for 10 minutes or until golden brown.

GRETNA

Helen Thigpen
JEFFERSON PARISH

Banana Split Surprize

SERVES 20

2 cups Graham Cracker crumbs
1 1/2 cups margarine
2 cups powdered sugar
2 eggs
5 bananas, sliced
1 (16 oz.) can crushed pineapple, drained
1 (4 oz.) jar cherries
1 (16 oz.) large container Cool Whip
1 cup pecans, chopped

Mix cracker crumbs with 1/2 cup melted margarine. Spread in a 14" X 9" X 2" pan. Cream 1 cup margarine and gradually add sugar. Add eggs one at a time, beating well after each. Spread mixture over cracker crumb crust. Top with sliced bananas. Top with drained pineapple. Spread Cool Whip over pineapple. Garnish with cherries and chopped pecans. Chill thoroughly. May be frozen. Better if served day after. Bon Appetite!

GROSSE TETE

Mrs. Philip D. Sarullo
IBERVILLE PARISH

Gobble Them Up Toffee Bars

SERVES SEVERAL

1 stick margarine
1 stick butter
1/2 cup sugar
1/2 cup chopped nuts
48 sections of graham crackers

Melt butter and margarine. Add sugar and bring to a boil, stirring 2 minutes. Pour over crackers placed on cookie sheet. Sprinkle with nuts. Bake at 325 degrees for 10 minutes. Remove and cool.

HAHNVILLE

Laurie S. Goodell
ST. CHARLES PARISH

49

No Cook Banana Pudding

SERVES 12

2 boxes French vanilla instant pudding
1 box banana creme instant pudding
5 cups milk
1 large container Cool Whip
5-6 bananas
1 large package vanilla wafers

Mix puddings with milk and blend in Cool Whip. Slice bananas and fold into pudding. Fold in the vanilla wafers gently. Chill and serve.

HAMMOND

Raine Himel
TANGIPAHOA PARISH

Delicious Oatmeal Cookies

MAKES 4 DOZEN

2 sticks butter
1 cup nuts
1 cup raisins
3 1/2 cups flour
2 cups oatmeal
3 eggs
2 cups sugar
5 tsp. water
1 tsp. vanilla
1 tsp. soda
Dash of cinnamon
Dash of nutmeg

Cream margarine and sugar. Add eggs one at a time, beating after each addition. Whip in the oatmeal, raisins and nuts. Dissolve soda in water and vanilla and add to mixture. Add flour and spices. Drop on cookie sheet. Bake at 325 degrees for 10-15 minutes. They will be slightly brown.

HARAHAN

Marian G. Ballard
JEFFERSON PARISH

Chess Cake

SERVES 20-36

1 box butter recipe cake mix
1 stick butter or margarine
4 eggs
1 (8 oz.) Philadelphia cream cheese
1 box confectioners sugar

Mix cake mix, butter and one egg in a bowl by hand until blended. Spread in a greased and floured 9" X 13" cake pan. Blend cream cheese, 3 eggs and 3/4 box of confectioners sugar on medium speed until creamy consistency. Pour over cake batter and place in a preheated 350 degree oven for 45 to 60 minutes.

HARDWOOD

Lucinda Brown
WEST FELICIANA PARISH

Dutch Apple Cake

SERVES 10-12

1 package Pillsbury lemon cake mix
1/2 cup butter or margarine, melted
2 eggs
2 cups sliced apples, drained
1 package Pillsbury coconut, pecan or almond frosting mix
1/4 cup butter or margarine, melted
Whipped Cream

In a large bowl, combine dry cake mix and 1/2 cup butter and eggs. Stir by hand until cake is moistened. Pat into ungreased 9"X 13" pan. Top with drained apples. Combine frosting and 1/4 cup butter. Sprinkle over apples. Bake at 350 degrees for 40 to 50 minutes or when toothpick comes out clean. Cool and top with whipped cream. Cut into squares.

HOUMA

Ann L. Melum
TERREBONNE PARISH

Banana Split Cake

SERVES 20-24

3 sticks margarine or butter
2 cups graham cracker crumbs
3 eggs
2 cups powdered sugar
4 ripe bananas, sliced
1 large can crushed pineapple, well drained
Chopped pecans
Chopped cherries
1 large container Cool Whip

Melt 1 stick margarine and mix with graham cracker crumbs. Put crumb mix in bottom of 13" X 9" X 2" pan. Beat the following with mixer for no less than 15 minutes: 3 eggs, 2 sticks margarine and 2 cups powdered sugar. Spread over crust. Cover with sliced bananas. Spread 1 large can crushed pineapple over this. Cover this with Cool Whip. Sprinkle with chopped cherries and pecans. Refrigerate at least 1 day before serving. It gets better with age.

INDEPENDENCE

Virginia G. Patanella
TANGIPAHOA PARISH

Pumpkin Dessert

SERVES 12-14

1 (12 oz.) can milk
3 eggs
1 cup sugar
1 tsp. vanilla
1 tsp. cinnamon
2 cups pumpkin (16 oz. can)
1 box yellow cake mix
1 1/2 cups chopped pecans
1 1/2 sticks butter or margarine, melted
TOPPING:
1 (8 oz.) package cream cheese, softened
1/2 cup powdered sugar
1 (12 oz.) container Cool Whip, thawed

Beat sugar, eggs, vanilla, cinnamon and milk together.
Blend in pumpkin. Pour into a greased 10" X 14" baking
dish. Sprinkle cake mix over this and then chopped pecans.
Drizzle melted butter over all. Bake for about 40 to 45
minutes in 350 degree oven. If pecans seem to be brown-
ing too fast, put a loose sheet of foil over dish. TOPPING:
Mix together cream cheese and powdered sugar until well
blended. Fold in Cool Whip thoroughly. Spread over top of
cooled dessert, then refrigerate.

INNIS

Zel Grezaffi
POINT COUPEE PARISH

Praline Cake

SERVES 16

1/2 cup butter
1 1/3 cups sugar
2 eggs, divided
1 cup milk
2 1/4 cups flour
2 1/2 tsp. baking powder
1/4 tsp. salt
1 tsp. vanilla
4 tbsp. burnt sugar syrup
Chopped pecans
BURNT SUGAR SYRUP:
1 cup sugar
1/2 cup boiling water
ICING:
2 cups sugar
2 tbsp. corn syrup
3/4 cup milk
1/4 tsp. salt
2 tbsp. butter
1 tbsp. vanilla
4 tbsp. burnt sugar syrup
Chopped pecans

Beat egg yolks and whites separately. Cream butter and sugar. Add egg yolks. Sift flour, baking powder and salt 3 times and add alternately with milk. Add vanilla and burnt sugar syrup. Fold in beaten egg whites. Pour batter in pans and sprinkle chopped pecans over top of dough. Bake at 350 degrees for 30 minutes for 2 layers or 45 minutes for 1 loaf. BURNT SUGAR SYRUP: In saucepan on high heat, stir sugar until melted and bubbles around edges. Remove from heat and slowly add water. Return to heat and stir until sugar thoroughly dissolves.

Should be the consistency of corn syrup. If too thick add a little water. If too thin boil a little longer. ICING: Stir sugar, corn syrup, salt and milk together and boil 3 minutes covered. Remove lid and cook to soft ball stage. Remove from heat, add butter and vanilla. Cool until lukewarm, beat until creamy. When too stiff to spread add burnt sugar syrup and pecans. Spread on cake.

JACKSON

Melba A. Wesley
EAST FELICIANA PARISH

Coconut Mound Cake

SERVES 8-10

1 box dark chocolate cake mix
1 (7 oz.) can Angel Flake coconut
1 (8.5 oz.) can Coco Lopez

Bake chocolate cake as directed on box, but bake in a bundt pan and cool. Remove carefully a section 1 1/2" wide by 2" deep from the top of the cake with a spoon. Try not to make center to wide or too deep. Mix 1/2 can Coco Lopez with coconut. Spoon mixture into cut section of cake. Pour remainder of Coco Lopez over coconut. Cover with chocolate icing and top with cherries.

KENNER

Sandy Autin
JEFFERSON PARISH

Rich and Creamy Squares

SERVES 24

BASE:
1 (18.25 oz.) box yellow or
   devil's food cake mix
2 eggs
1/2 cup butter, melted
1 tbsp. milk
1/2 cup pecans, chopped

TOPPING:
1 (8 oz.) package cream
   cheese, softened
2 eggs
3 1/2 cups confectioners sugar
1 tsp. vanilla

Heat oven to 350 degrees. Grease 13" X 9" X 2" pan.
BASE: Combine cake mix, 2 eggs, melted butter, milk and
nuts in a large bowl. Mix with fork or at low speed of electric mixer until cake mix is just moistened. Pour into pan.
Spread evenly. TOPPING: Beat cream cheese in large bowl
at medium speed of electric mixer until smooth. Beat in 2
eggs, sugar and vanilla until smooth. Spread evenly over
base. Bake at 350 degrees for 35 minutes. Edges and top
will be light golden brown and will have a slightly shiny
appearance. Cool completely. Cut into squares about
1 1/2" X 1 1/2". Makes about 4 dozen bars.

KENTWOOD

Jennifer L. Meyn
TANGIPAHOA PARISH

Out Of This World Dessert

SERVES 10-12

CRUST:
1 stick butter, room temperature
1/2 cup powdered sugar
1 cup flour
1 cup pecans, chopped
FILLING:
2 (8 oz.) packages Philadelphia Cream Cheese
2 cups powdered sugar
2 cups Cool Whip
1 tbsp. vanilla
2 boxes instant vanilla pudding
2 boxes instant chocolate pudding
4 1/2 cups cold milk

CRUST: Mix butter, powdered sugar and flour. Add pecans and spread on bottom of 9" X 13" pan. Bake at 350 degrees for 25 minutes then cool. FIRST LAYER: Mix cream cheese, powdered sugar, Cool Whip and vanilla. Spread over crust. SECOND LAYER: Mix puddings with milk and spread over cream cheese. Top with Cool Whip and refrigerate.

LABADIEVILLE

Darlene Bernard
ASSUMPTION PARISH

Apple Crisp

SERVES 6

5 cups apples, peeled and sliced
1 cup uncooked oatmeal
1/2 cup brown sugar
1/2 cup melted butter
1/3 cup all-purpose flour

Preheat oven to 375 degrees. Put apples in an 8" square pan. Combine the rest of the ingredients, mixing until crumbly. Sprinkle on top of apples. Bake for 30 to 45 minutes until apples are tender. Can be served as is or over vanilla ice cream.

LAPLACE

Jeri Este' Landry
ST. JOHN THE BAPTIST PARISH

Sour Cream Pound Cake

SERVES 25

3 cups sugar
6 eggs
1/4 tsp. salt
1 cup sour cream
3 sticks butter
3 cups plain flour
1/4 tsp. baking soda
2 tsp. vanilla

Cream butter and sugar together until light and fluffy. Beat in eggs one at a time. Sift flour, soda and salt together. Add the dry ingredients to the cake batter. Alternating with the sour cream. Add vanilla and pour into a well greased and floured 10" tube pan (or 2 loaf pans). Bake at 315 degrees for about 90 minutes.

LIVINGSTON

Ms. Donnie Duffy
LIVINGSTON PARISH

Lightning Cake

SERVES 12

1 1/2 cups ground almonds or pecans
1/2 lb. butter
1/2 lb. flour
3/4 lb. sugar + 1 cup for topping
4 large eggs
1 1/2 tsp. vanilla

Cream butter. Add sugar and flour. Add eggs, one at a time. Add vanilla. Spread on well greased cookie sheet that has about a 3/4" ledge. Mix ground nuts with 1 cup sugar and sprinkle generously on top of mixture. Bake at 350 degrees for about 10 to 20 minutes, until barely golden brown. Cool in pan and cut into diamonds.

LIVONIA

Tania Marie Joffrion
POINTE COUPEE PARISH

Taffy Apple Dessert

SERVES 8-10

2 cups chunk pineapple (save juice)
2 cups mini marshmallows
2 cups diced apples
1/2 cup Spanish peanuts
1 tbsp. flour
1 egg yolk
1/2 cup sugar
1 1/2 tbsp. white vinegar
1 (8 oz.) container Cool Whip

Mix first 4 ingredients and set aside. Cook pineapple juice, flour, egg yolk, sugar and vinegar until thickened. When mix is slightly cooled, add Cool Whip and gently blend together until smooth. Fold the creamy mixture over the pineapple and apples and chill a minimum of 6 hours or over night. Tastes like caramel apples.

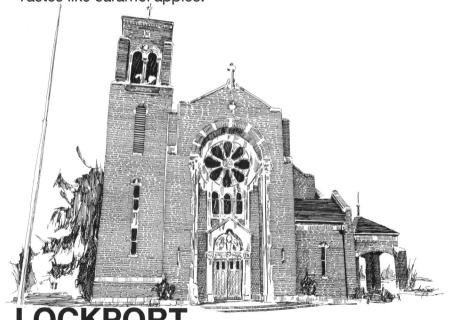

LOCKPORT

Joyce Souther
LAFOURCHE PARISH

Quick And Easy Peach Cobbler

SERVES 4

1 cup "reduced fat" Bisquick
1/2 cup sugar
1/2 cup water
1 can sliced peaches
2 tbsp. margarine
Ground cinnamon

Mix Bisquick, water and sugar. Pour into baking pan. Add peaches. Dot with margarine and sprinkle cinnamon on top. Bake in 400 degree oven for 25 minutes.

LULING

Florence Pitre
ST. CHARLES PARISH

Date Pecan Balls

MAKES 3 DOZEN

1 cup (2 sticks) soft butter
1/4 cup sugar
2 tsp. vanilla
2 cups all-purpose flour
2 cups finely ground pecans
1 (8 oz.) package diced dates
Powdered sugar

Cream butter and sugar, add vanilla and flour, and mix lightly. Add pecans and dates and mix until well blended. Shape into balls using about 1 heaping teaspoon per ball. Refrigerate for 1 to 2 hours. Place 1 inch apart on ungreased cookie sheet and bake in preheated 350 degree oven for 20 minutes or until very lightly browned. Remove from oven and roll at once in powdered sugar. Makes about 3 dozen.

LUTCHER

Jean Wahl
ST. JAMES PARISH

The "Best" Fudge

MAKES 36 PIECES

4 cups sugar
3 squares chocolate
1/4 cup white syrup
1 1/3 cups milk
5 tbsp. butter
1 tsp. vanilla
1 cup chopped nuts

Combine sugar, chocolate, syrup and milk over low heat. Stir while increasing heat to medium and stir until sugar dissolves. Keep on medium heat and then cook without stirring to 236 degrees or soft ball stage. Remove from heat and add butter but don't stir. Cool to about 150 degrees, then beat until smooth and dull looking. Add vanilla and nuts.

MADISONVILLE

Michelle Owens
ST. TAMMANY PARISH

Lemon Pound Cake

SERVES 8

1 package yellow or
 lemon cake mix
1 package lemon instant
 pudding (4 serving size)
1/2 cup Crisco oil
1 cup water
4 eggs
1 tsp. lemon flavoring

TOPPING:
1 stick margarine
1 cup sugar
1/4 cup water
1/2 cup lemon juice
1 tsp. lemon flavoring
GLAZE:
1 cup powdered sugar
2 tbsp. lemon juice

CRUST: Blend all cake ingredients in a bowl. Beat 2 minutes. Spray bundt pan with Pam. Pour in mixture and bake at 350 degrees for 45-55 minutes. TOPPING: Cook margarine, sugar, water and lemon juice until melted and blended. Add lemon flavoring to the mixture and then spoon over hot cake as soon as it comes out of the oven. Let cake set in pan for 30 minutes and then turn into a plate. GLAZE: Blend powdered sugar and lemon juice. Drizzle over top of cake when cooled.

MANDEVILLE

Betty Pellegrin
ST.TAMMANY PARISH

Cracker Custard

SERVES 6-8

1/3 cup sugar
2 egg yolks
2 1/2 cups milk
4 tbsp. butter, softened
1 tsp. vanilla extract
1 package unsalted crackers
MERINGUE:
2 egg whites
4 tbsp. sugar

Pour sugar, egg yolks and milk in pot. Stir and bring to a
boil. Take off stove as soon as it comes to a boil. Pour into
a dish. Add butter and mix until melted. Add vanilla extract.
Take crackers, a few at a time and crumble by hand into
bowl. With spoon, spread evenly in liquid mixture in 1 1/2
qt. oblong pyrex dish and saturate. For meringue beat egg
whites until stiff. Gradually add sugar, 2 tbsp. for each egg
white, beating after each addition. Beat until meringue
stands in firm peaks. Spread over top of custard and bake
in 350 degree oven until meringue is lightly browned.

MARINGOUIN

Lynette Thibodeaux
IBERVILLE PARISH

Aunt Mary's Strawberry Cake

SERVES 20-24

1 box white cake mix,
  Duncan Hines
4 eggs
1 cup oil
1/2 cup crushed strawberries
1/2 cup coconut
1/2 cup pecans, chopped
1 small box strawberry gelatin

TOPPING:
1/2 cup crushed strawberries
3/4 cup coconut
1/2 cup pecans, chopped
1/2 stick margarine
1/2 to 3/4 lb. confectioners
  sugar

Combine first 4 ingredients and gelatin. Mix well with electric mixer. Slowly add coconut and pecans. Pour into 13" X 9" pan and bake 35 to 40 minutes. When cake is baked, remove from oven and cool slightly. Slowly spoon icing on warm cake being careful not to crumble top of cake.
TOPPING: Combine sugar, margarine and strawberries. Stir in coconut and pecans. Adjust sugar or strawberries so topping is easily spooned on warm cake.

MAUREPAS

Linda K. Ivanyisky
LIVINGSTON PARISH

Heavenly Pound Cake

SERVES 12

1 lb. butter, softened
3 cups sugar
6 eggs
4 cups all-purpose flour
3/4 cup milk
1 tsp. vanilla
1 tsp. almond
1/2 cup cocoa
Dust of mace

Cream butter and sugar on medium speed. Add eggs, one at a time, beating after each addition. Add flour and cocoa to creamed mixture alternately with milk, beginning and ending with flour. Mix until blended after each addition. Stir in flavorings. Pour batter into greased and floured 10" tube pan. Bake at 300 degrees for 1 hour and 40 minutes. Cool in pan 15 minutes, remove and cool on rack.

METAIRIE

Kay McGinley
JEFFERSON PARISH

Mandarin Orange Cake

SERVES 12

1 box yellow cake mix
1/2 cup sugar
4 eggs
3/4 cup oil
1 can Mandarin oranges, including juice
ICING:
1 large box instant vanilla pudding
1 large can crushed pineapple
1 large container Cool Whip
1 cup pecans

Combine cake mix, sugar, eggs and oil and mix well. Add Manderin oranges and fold in. Pour into three cake pans and bake at 350 degrees until done. ICING: Combine vanilla pudding and crushed pineapple. Mix well and let stand for 15 minutes. Fold in Cool Whip and pecans. Frost layers. Keep refrigerated.

MONTPELIER

Ione King
ST. HELENA PARISH

Strawberry Cream Cheese Pie

SERVES 8

1 (9") graham cracker shell
1 (8 oz.) cream cheese
1 (8 oz.) carton sour cream

3 pts. fresh strawberries or
  2 (10 oz.) boxes frozen
  strawberries
3 tbsp. cornstarch
1/8 tsp. vanilla

Blend cream cheese with 1/2 of the sour cream. Measure 1/2 cup of mixture and spread over bottom of shell. Set the rest aside. Crush 1 pt. fresh strawberries and sprinkle with 1/4 cup sugar and let stand until very juicy. Press gently through a sieve, measure juice, then add enough water to make 1 1/2 cups. Mix in cornstarch, heat on low to medium and stir until thick, about 10 minutes. Set aside to cool. When cool pour a thin layer into shell and add other berries (whole or cut.) Top with rest of sauce and chill. Add 1 tbsp. sugar, the rest of the sour cream and 1/8 tsp. vanilla to remainder of cream cheese mixture. Garnish pie as desired. * To use frozen berries, thaw and measure 1 1/2 cups of syrup by straining. Add water if necessary. Mix 1/4 cup cornstarch and heat until sauce is thick, then cook 5 minutes more. Cool and fold in berries and syrup. Mix gently. Pour into shell. Chill and garnish. It's worth the trouble.

MORGANZA

Diane R. Grantham
POINTE COUPEE PARISH

Hello Dolly's

SERVES 12-15

1 stick butter or margarine
1 1/2 cups graham cracker crumbs
1 cup chopped pecans
1 (16 oz.) package Nestle's semi sweet chocolate or
   1 (6 oz.) package Nestle's butterscotch flavored morsels
1 (3 1/2 oz.) can flaked coconut
1 can Magnolia Brand sweetened condensed milk

Pour melted butter or margarine in bottom of 13"X 9"X 2" pan. Sprinkle cracker crumbs evenly over melted butter or margarine. Sprinkle chopped pecans evenly over crumbs. Scatter chocolate or butterscotch morsels over pecans. Sprinkle coconut over morsels. Pour condensed milk evenly over coconut. Bake at 350 degrees until lightly brown on top. Cool in pan for 15 minutes. Cut into bars.

NAPOLEONVILLE

Mrs. Theresa Simoneaux
ASSUMPTION PARISH

Praline Sauce

MAKES 5 CUPS

2 cups white corn syrup
2 cups dark corn syrup
1/2 cup cane syrup
2 cups pecans, halves or pieces
1/2 cup sugar
1/2 cup water
1 tsp. vanilla

Combine dark and light corn syrup, pecans, cane syrup, sugar and water in a sauce pan. Bring to a boil. Remove from heat and cool. Serve over ice cream, cheese cake or pound cake. Can be stored in the refrigerator. Try praline sauce on waffles, french toast, pancakes or biscuits for an added taste of the south.

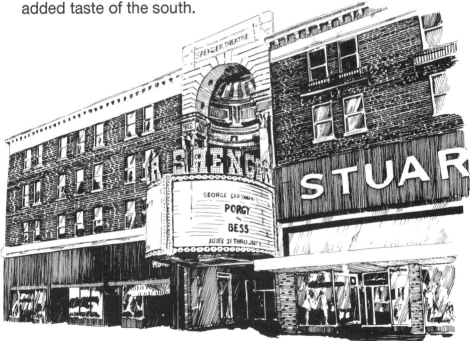

NEW ORLEANS

Susan Murphy
ORLEANS PARISH

75

Parlange Plantation Pudding

SERVES 6

1 1/4 cups brown sugar
3 1/4 tbsp. white whole wheat flour
2 pinches of salt
3 1/4 tbsp. butter
1 cup sweet milk
2 egg yolks
2 egg whites
Juice of 1 1/2 lemons

Mix butter, flour, brown sugar and salt together. Add lemon juice, beaten egg yolks and milk. Beat egg whites and add to mixture. Pour into custard cups. Put the cups in a pan of warm water, 1/2" deep. Bake at 300 degrees for 1 1/2 hours. Serve while warm. NOTE: Regular cake flour can be used when whole wheat flour is unavailable.

NEW ROADS

Lucy Brandon Parlange
POINTE COUPEE PARISH

Coconut Cream Cake

SERVES 12

2 cups sugar
1 stick butter
1/2 cup Crisco
5 egg yolks
1 cup buttermilk
1 tsp. soda
1 cup flaked coconut
2 cups flour
1 tsp. vanilla
Pecans for top, optional

ICING:
1 stick butter
1 (8 oz.) package cream cheese
1 tsp. vanilla
1 box powdered sugar

Cream together sugar, butter and Crisco. Add buttermilk, soda and coconut. Add egg yolks, one at a time. Add flour. Beat 5 egg whites until stiff. Add 1 tsp. vanilla. Fold into mixture. Pour into 3 greased and floured 9" pans. Bake at 325 degrees for 35 minutes. Cool, then ice. Mix together butter, cream cheese, powdered sugar and vanilla. Mix well. Put between layers and on top and sides of cake.

NORCO

Catherine Dufresne
ST. CHARLES PARISH

Stack Cake

SERVES 10-12

2 3/4 cups flour
2 tsp. cloves
2 tsp. allspice
2 tsp. baking powder
1 tsp. nutmeg
1/2 tsp. baking soda

6 eggs, separated
2 cups sugar, divided
2 sticks oleo, softened
1/2 cup sour cream
2 cups seedless blackberry jam

Grease six 9" pans and line with paper. In small bowl, combine first 6 ingredients and set aside. In large bowl, beat egg whites until foamy, gradually beat in 1/4 cup sugar. Beat until stiff peaks form and set aside. In another bowl, beat oleo and remaining 1 3/4 cups sugar until light and fluffy, about 5 minutes. Add egg yolks and sour cream and beat 3 more minutes. At low speed, beat in flour mixture just until blended. With spatula, fold in about 1 cup of egg whites. Gently fold remainder of whites into batter. Spread about 1 cup of batter into each baking pan. Bake 20 minutes at 300 degrees. When cool, assemble all six layers on plate with jam spread between each layer and on top.

NORWOOD

Brenda F. DeValcourt
EAST FELICIANA PARISH

Cracker Pudding

SERVES 10-12

6 egg yolks
2 cups sugar
1 block margarine
2 cans Pet milk
2 cups water
2 packs unsalted crackers
2 tsp. vanilla
6 egg whites

In a 9" X 11" glass baking dish cream egg yolks, sugar and margarine. Add vanilla, Pet milk and water. Mix well. Break crackers into mixture. With 6 egg whites make meringue. Bake at 300 degrees for about 30 to 40 minutes or until meringue gets golden brown.

PIERRE PART

Stephanie M. Sedotal
ASSUMPTION PARISH

79

"Gone With The Wind" Slice Cake

SERVES 12

1 cup shortening
2 cups sugar
3 1/2 cups plain flour
1 tsp. soda
2 tsp. grated orange rind
4 eggs
1/2 cup buttermilk
1 package dates,
  cut in half

1 cup Angle Flake coconut
1 cup chopped pecans
2 cups orange slice candy, cut up
  and dredged in 1/2 cup flour

ICING:
1 cup powdered sugar
1/2 cup orange juice
2 tsp. grated orange rind

Hand mix all ingredients. Cream shortening, sugar and eggs. Add soda to buttermilk. Stir and fold into creamed shortening along with flour and all fruit, coconut and pecans. Add grated orange rind, then mix by hand. Makes a stiff dough. Put into large bundt pan or tube pan, greased and floured. Bake at 250 degrees for 3 hours. Spread icing over hot cake when done. Let sit in pan until cold, then remove. This makes a very large, rich delicious cake. It is gone with the wind fast.

PINE GROVE

Fay B. Rollinson
ST. HELENA PARISH

Orange Mist Chocolate Cheesecake
SERVES 10-12

1 1/2 cups chocolate wafer crumbs
3 tbsp. sugar
1/4 cup margarine, melted
3 (8 oz.) packages cream cheese
2/3 cup sugar
3 eggs
1 (6 oz.) package semisweet chocolate pieces, melted
1/3 cup sour cream
2 tbsp. orange flavored liqueur

Combine crumbs, sugar and margarine. Press into bottom of 9" spring form pan. Bake at 350 degrees for 10 minutes. Combine cream cheese and sugar, mixing at medium speed on electric mixer until well blended. Add eggs, one at a time, mixing well after each addition. Blend in chocolate pieces, sour cream and liqueur. Pour over crust. Bake at 350 degrees for 50 minutes. Loosen cake from rim of pan. Cool before removing rim of pan. Chill. Garnish with whipped cream and grated orange peel.

PLAQUEMINE

Kathy Stafford
IBERVILLE PARISH

Blueberry Cake

SERVES 15

1 box of butter cake mix
3 eggs
1 (8 oz.) softened cream cheese
1/2 cup water
1/2 cup oil
1 cup blueberries, fresh or frozen
1/4 cup flour
ICING:
2 cups confectioners sugar
2 tbsp. plus 2 tsp. lemon juice
2 tbsp. oil

Mix the cake mix, eggs, cream cheese, water and oil together with a blender. In a pan, roll the blueberries in the flour. Add floured blueberries to the mixture and stir. Pour mixture into a 9" X 13" pan that has been oiled and floured. Bake at 350 degrees for 1 hour. ICING: Add all of the icing ingredients together and mix. Spread over cooled cake.

PONCHATOULA

Mary Ann Cooper
TANGIPAHOA PARISH

Frozen Lemon Squares

SERVES 10-12

1/4 cup butter or margarine, melted
1 1/4 cups graham cracker crumbs
1/4 cup sugar
3 egg yolks
1 can Eagle Brand sweetened condensed milk
3/4 cup Realemon lemon juice
Cool Whip

Combine margarine, crumbs, and sugar. Press into 8" or 9" square pan. In bowl, beat egg yolks. Stir in sweetened condensed milk and Realemon. Pour into crust. Top with Cool Whip. Freeze until firm. Cut into squares.

PORT ALLEN

Deby Hebert
WEST BATON ROUGE PARISH

Banana Split Dessert

SERVES 16-20

2 eggs
4 sticks margarine
5 or 6 medium bananas
1 large carton Cool Whip
1 small jar red cherries, halved
2 cups confectioner sugar
2 cups graham cracker crumbs
1 large can crushed pineapple
1 cup chopped pecans

Melt 2 sticks of margarine and mix with the graham cracker crumbs. Line the bottom af a 13" X 9" pan. Mix the eggs, 2 sticks of margarine and sugar no less than 15 minutes. Spread mixture over graham cracker lining. Slice the bananas over the mixture and cover with the drained pineapple. Top with Cool Whip, then sprinkle with the pecans and cherries. Refrigerate overnight.

PORT SULPHUR

Judy W. Kodrin
PLAQUEMINES PARISH

84

Milk Pie

SERVES 8

FILLING:
3 cups milk
1 cup sugar
1/2 cup flour
2 eggs
1 tsp. vanilla
Dash of nutmeg

CRUST:
1 stick margarine, softened
3/4 cup sugar
1 egg
2 cups flour
1/2 tsp. baking soda
1/4 tsp. salt

For custard filling, heat milk on a low temperature. Mix sugar, flour and eggs. Beat well and pour into heated milk. Cook over medium heat until mixture boils. Remove from heat, and add vanilla and nutmeg. For sweet crust, beat together margarine and sugar. Beat in egg. Sift together flour, baking soda and salt and add to sugar mixture. Roll 3/4 of the dough out on a floured pastry cloth the size of a 10 in. pie pan. Place crust in pan. Pour custard into pre-pared crust. Roll out remaining dough and cut into long narrow strips. Lay strips across pie. Bake at 350 degrees for 15 to 20 minutes or until slightly brown. Cool and serve. Refrigerate after serving.

PORT VINCENT

Katie Jenks
LIVINGSTON PARISH

Heavenly Hash Cake

SERVES 12

2 sticks oleo
4 eggs
2 cups sugar
2 tsp. vanilla
1 1/2 cups self-rising flour
4 tbsp. cocoa
1 1/2 cups chopped pecans
ICING:
1 box powdered sugar
1 stick oleo
4 tbsp. cocoa
1/4 cup cream
16 marshmallows

Melt oleo at room temperature. Beat eggs and sugar together. Stir in oleo and vanilla. Sift flour and cocoa together and fold into the mixture. Add pecans. Pour into a greased and floured 13" X 9" pan. Bake in oven at 350 degrees for 40 minutes. Cut marshmallows in half and place on top of cake while it is still hot. Mix icing ingredients and spread on cake while it is still hot.

PRAIRIEVILLE

Lee Gautreaux
ASCENSION PARISH

Clara's Cheese Cake

SERVES 6-8

CRUST:
1 (12 oz.) box vanilla wafers
1/4 lb. (1 stick) butter
2/3 cup chopped pecans
CHEESE LAYER:
3 (8 oz.) packages of cream cheese
1 cup sugar
3 eggs
1/2 tsp. vanilla
SOUR CREAM MIXTURE:
1 pint sour cream
3 tbsp. sugar
1/2 tsp. vanilla
1 can fruit pie filling

Crush wafers. Mix in melted butter and nuts. Press around bottom and sides of spring form pan. Mix cream cheese with sugar. Add eggs, one at a time, then vanilla. Spoon into crust. Bake 30 minutes at 375 degrees. Take out immediately. Beat together and put the sour cream mixture onto cheese layer; bake 5 minutes at 500 degrees. Cool. Spread on top, 1 can fruit pie filling and chill.

RACELAND

Clara B. Theriot
LAFOURCHE PARISH

Pecan Cocoons

SERVES 30

1 1/4 sticks butter, melted
4 tbsp. sugar
1 tbsp. ice water
1 tbsp. vanilla extract
2 cups plain flour
2 cups pecans, chopped fine
1 cup confectioners sugar

Mix in order given until dough is mixed well. Fold in nut meat by hand. Shape into cocoons with hands and place on greased pan. Bake in 250 degree oven for 1 hour. Dust with powdered sugar while hot. This makes 30 cocoons 1 1/2" long.

REILEY

Carol Giffin
EAST FELICIANA PARISH

Maw's Bouillie (Custard)

SERVES 6

2 cans Pet evaporated milk
1 can water (use Pet milk can)
2 tbsp. sugar
2 tbsp. vanilla
3 egg yolks
3 tbsp. corn starch
1/2 cup cool tap water
12 or more vanilla wafers

Beat by hand, 3 egg yolks in a small bowl. Mix corn starch and cool water. (The water keeps the cornstarch from making lumps.) Pour cornstarch liquid into egg yolk mixture and stir well. Add sugar and vanilla and stir well. Combine milk and tap water in pot and bring to a boil, approximately 10 minutes. Reduce heat and gradually pour in cornstarch and egg mixture to milk stirring slowly. Remove from heat and add 10 or more vanilla wafers to custard. This is not a thick custard and it can be served hot or cold. Custard can be spooned over pound cake or it can be frozen to make ice cream. Coconut or bananas can be added.

RESERVE

Mrs. Eola Boe' Weber
ST. JOHN THE BAPTIST PARISH

Bayou Brownies

SERVES 16

1 box yellow butter cake mix
1 egg, beaten
1 stick butter
1 tbsp. water
1 box powdered sugar
3 eggs
1 (8 oz.) package cream cheese, softened

Mix cake mix, 1 egg, butter and water until it forms a stiff dough. With buttered fingers, press dough into a 13" X 9" X 2" greased pan. Blend powdered sugar, 3 eggs and cream cheese until smooth and pour over dough. Bake at 350 to 375 degrees for 45 minutes. Top will be golden brown. Cool before cutting.

ROSEDALE

Brenda Lewis
IBERVILLE PARISH

Aunt Jimmie's Fudge Cake

SERVES 10-12

2 sticks margarine
2 cups sugar
1/2 cup cocoa
1 cup flour
1 cup pecans, chopped
4 eggs
1 tsp. vanilla
ICING:
2 cups confectioner sugar
1 tsp. vanilla
1/4 cup cocoa
4 tbsp. margarine
2 tbsp. cream or milk

Cream sugar, cocoa and margarine well. Add eggs, one at a time, then flour. Beat all together. Add vanilla and nuts. Pour into greased 9" X 13" pan and bake at 300 degrees for about 35 minutes. Test with toothpick. Immediately after removing from the oven, pour on chocolate icing. ICING: Heat margarine and cocoa in saucepan. Gradually beat in confectioners sugar and milk alternately. Add vanilla.

SLAUGHTER

Jan Chandler
EAST FELICIANA PARISH

Meresie's Sunday Treat

SERVES 4-6

1 can Eagle Brand condensed milk
1/2 cup fresh squeezed lemon juice
1/2 pt. whipping cream
1-2 doz. lady fingers
Vanilla extract
1/3 cup sugar

Line casserole dish with lady fingers, (rounded edges out).
Mix Eagle Brand milk and lemon juice until thick and pour
over lady fingers. Whip cream into peaks and add sugar
and real vanilla to taste. Top the condensed milk and lemon
juice mixture and enjoy. Serve in parfait glasses.

SLIDELL

Mrs. Sue Ribbeck Wagner/Honey Island Swamp
ST. TAMMANY PARISH

Orange Slice Cake
SERVES 12

1 cup shortening
1 tsp. soda
1/4 cup buttermilk
1 package chopped dates
1 cup coconut
4 eggs
2 cups sugar
2 1/2 cups flour
1 package oranges slices (candy)
2 cups pecans
ICING:
1 cup fresh orange juice
2 cups powdered sugar

Cream shortening and sugar. Add eggs, one at a time. Mix 2 cups flour and soda. Add milk, chopped dates and orange slices, chopped fine with 1/2 cup flour. Add coconut and pecans. Fold into batter. Bake in tube pan for 2 1/2 hours at 225 degrees. Mix ingredients for icing and pour over cake.

SORRENTO

Janice P. LeBlanc
ASCENSION PARISH

93

Bartlett Amandine Mousse

SERVES 2

1/4 cup cold water
1 env. unflavored gelatin
1/4 cup boiling water
1 fresh ripe pear, peeled
2/3 cup instant non-fat dry powdered milk
1 capful almond extract
Artificial sweetener to equal 6 tsp. sugar
6-8 ice cubes

Sprinkle gelatin over cold water to soften; add boiling water. Pour gelatin mixture into blender. Add 3/4 of the pear, dry milk powder, extract and sweetener. Blend until smooth. Add ice cubes, one at a time, blending after each addition. Cut remaining 1/4 of pear into finely diced pieces and fold into blended mixture. Pour mousse mixture into dessert glasses. Serve immediately, or chill as desired.

THE
General Store
294-3229

ICE

ICE
ICE

SPRINGFIELD

Mitsie Sue Creel
LIVINGSTON PARISH

Old Fashioned Cream Puffs

SERVES 12-15

1 cup water
1/2 cup butter or margarine
1 tsp. sugar
1/4 tsp. salt
1 cup plain flour
4 eggs

Heat water, butter, sugar and salt to a rolling boil in sauce-pan. Add flour all at once and stir vigorously with a wooden spoon until thick and smooth (about 1 minute) staying away from sides. Remove from heat and add eggs one at a time, beating well after each egg. Use a wooden spoon or electric mixer until paste is shiny and smooth. Drop by tablespoonsful onto ungreased cookie sheet and bake at 400 degrees for about 20 to 30 minutes. Let cool, then fill each cream puff with instant pudding, either chocolate or vanilla.

ST. BERNARD

Mr. and Mrs. Robert A. Mallu Sr.
ST. BERNARD PARISH

7-Up Pound Cake

SERVES 12

3 cups sugar
3 sticks margarine
5 eggs
Dash of salt
1 tbsp. lemon juice
1 tsp. vanilla
1 tsp. almond extract
3 cups flour
7 oz. 7-Up

GLAZE:
1 cup powdered sugar
2 tbsp. margarine, melted
2 tbsp. lemon juice
1/2 tsp. almond extract

Grease tube pan or two loaf pans. Preheat oven to 325 degrees. Cream sugar and margarine. Add eggs, one at a time, beating well each time. Add lemon juice, vanilla and almond extract and beat well. Add flour and 7-Up alternating and beating well. Bake in tube pan or loaf pans for 1 hour and 15 minutes or longer. Mix the glaze and apply while the cake is still warm.

ST. FRANCISVILLE

Judy Decoteau
WEST FELICIANA PARISH

Chocolate Decadence

SERVES 6-8

1/2 stick butter, softened
1/3 cup sugar
1 tbsp. flour
1 cup finely chopped pecans
1 stick butter
1 cup sugar
2 oz. unsweetened chocolate, melted

1/8 tsp. salt
1/4 cup flour
2 eggs, beaten
1 tsp. vanilla
1 qt. vanilla ice cream, softened
1 cup Kahlua

Preheat oven to 325 degrees. Use a 9" pie plate. Combine first 4 ingredients and press into sides and bottom of pie plate. Cream butter and sugar, add next 5 ingredients, mix well and pour into pie crust. Bake 35 to 40 minutes or until filling is set. DO NOT OVERBAKE. Ice cream topping - Stir Kahlua into ice cream. Put into plastic container and freeze. To serve, pie should be warm or at room temperature. Stir ice cream well and spoon over each slice of pie.

THIBODAUX

Mary Alice Richard
LAFOURCHE PARISH

Date Balls

SERVES 20

2 sticks butter
1 lb. chopped dates
1 can coconut
2 cups chopped pecans
1 cup dark brown sugar
4 cups Rice Krispies
Powdered sugar

Cook butter, dates, coconut and sugar over low heat until bubbly for 6 minutes. Remove from heat. Add Rice Krispies and pecans, while stirring. Mix well. Roll into balls and coat with powdered sugar.

TICKFAW

Vickie Baiamonte
TANGIPAHOA PARISH

Oak Alley Restaurant's Special Bread Pudding with Whiskey Sauce

SERVES 24

8 cups sugar	10-12 po-boy bread (hoagies)
10 eggs	Cinnamon, optional
10 cups milk	1 cup sugar
1/2 cup vanilla	2 cups water
3/4 cup raisins	1/4 lb. butter
1/2 lb. butter	1/2 cup whiskey

Combine first 6 ingredients in a large mixing bowl. Tear bread into bite size pieces and add to mixture. Pour into large baking dish and bake at 350 degrees for 1 1/2 hours. Sprinkle cinnamon to taste.

WHISKEY SAUCE: Boil water, sugar and butter for 30 minutes. Add whiskey and remove from heat. Pour over warm bread pudding.

VACHERIE

Ellen A. Pitre/Oak Alley Restaurant
ST. JAMES PARISH

Red, White and Blueberry Bars
SERVES 12

1 (14 oz.) can condensed milk
1/3 cup lime juice
2 tsp. grated lime peel
2 cups miniature marshmallows

2 cups plain yogurt
1 pt. strawberries, sliced
1 pt. blueberries

In a large bowl combine the sweetened condensed milk, lime juice, grated lime peel and marshmallows. Put half the mixture into a 13" X 9" baking pan. Arrange half of the strawberries and blueberries over this, then cover with the remaining milk mixture and the rest of the fruit. Cover well with foil and place in the freezer until firm. Remove 10 minutes before cutting.

VARNADO

Jackie Ezell
WASHINGTON PARISH

Merlitone Pie

SERVES 12-16

6 to 8 merlitones
1 can cream
2 eggs
1 tbsp. vanilla
1/4 cup margarine, melted
1 small pack Jiffy Cake Mix
1 can Angle Flake Coconut

Boil merlitones until tender, about one hour. Drain, peel and mash. Mix cream, eggs, vanilla and margarine and mix well. Add cake mix and coconut. Grease a 9" X 13" cake pan. Cook at 350 degrees for 55 to 60 minutes. Check often.

VIOLET

Viola T. Dufrene
ST. BERNARD PARISH

Cake That Won't Last

SERVES 12

3 eggs, beaten
1 tsp. salt
1 tsp. soda
1 1/2 tsp. vanilla
3 cups flour
3 cups sugar
1 tsp. cinnamon
1 cup oil
2 cups bananas, cut into pieces
1/2 cup nuts
1 (8 oz.) can crushed pineapple and juice

Mix all ingredients together by hand. Pour into greased and floured Bundt pan. Bake at 350 degrees for 1 hour. Bake on top rack of oven.

WALKER

Ella Stokes
LIVINGSTON PARISH

Mom's Peach Stuff

SERVES 12-15

2 sticks butter
2 cups flour
1 cup chopped pecans
1 (8 oz.) container cream cheese
1 large size Cool Whip
1 cup powdered sugar
1 (3 oz.) package peach Jello mix
1 (3 oz.) package French vanilla instant pudding
1 1/2 cups milk
3 cups fresh or canned peaches

FIRST LAYER: Melt 2 sticks butter and stir in 2 cups flour. Spread over the bottom of a large Pyrex dish. Add 1 cup chopped pecans. Press into dough. Bake at 350 degrees for 15 to 20 minutes (until golden brown). Let cool completely. SECOND LAYER: Mix together cream cheese, 1/2 of the Cool Whip, and powdered sugar. Spread over crust. THIRD LAYER: In one bowl mix together Jello, 1 cup boiling water and 1/2 cup cold water. In a separate bowl mix together instant pudding, 1 1/2 cups milk, 3 cups fresh or canned peaches. (drain and use the juice with the Jello mix if using canned) Mix pudding and peaches with Jello mixture. Spread over second layer and cover with remaining Cool Whip.

WHITE CASTLE

Kay Russell
IBERVILLE PARISH

Lemon Squares

SERVES 12

CRUST:
1 cup butter, melted
2 cups sifted flour
1/2 cup powdered sugar
1/4 tsp. salt
TOPPING:
4 eggs, beaten
2 cups granulated sugar
4 tbsp. sifted flour
5 tbsp. lemon juice
1 1/2 tbsp. grated lemon rind
Powdered sugar

Mix crust ingredients and pat into bottom of 13" X 9" baking pan. Bake at 350 degrees for 20 minutes. Mix topping ingredients and pour on top of baked crust. Put back into 350 degree oven for 25 to 30 minutes. When cool, sprinkle with powdered sugar and cut into squares.

WHITEHALL

Brenda Bantaa
LIVINGSTON PARISH

Fudge Ribbon Parfaits

SERVES 8-12

1/2 lb. marshmallows
2 (1 oz.) squares unsweetened chocolate
1 (6 oz.) can evaporated milk
1 tsp. vanilla
1 qt. vanilla ice cream
1 pt. chocolate ice cream
Whipped cream
Cherries

In double boiler heat marshmallows, chocolate and 2 tbsp. of milk, stirring frequently until blended. Remove from heat. Gradually stir in remaining milk and vanilla. Cool. In chilled parfait glasses, alternate fudge sauce, vanilla ice cream and chocolate ice cream. Top with "fluffs" of whipped cream and cherries.

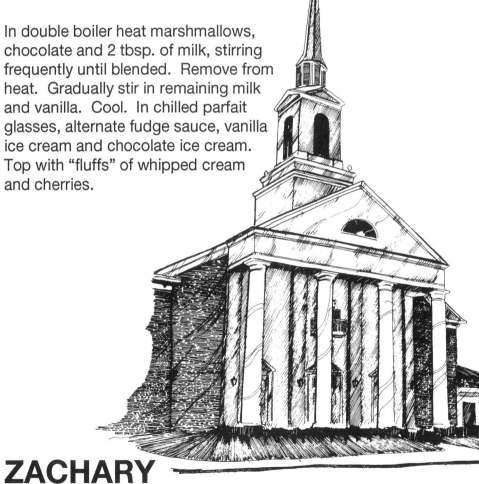

ZACHARY

Millie R. Odom
EAST BATON ROUGE PARISH

Southwest Section

Abbeville
Amelia
Baldwin
Berwick
Breaux Bridge
Cameron
Centerville
Church Point
Crowley
Delcambre
DeQuincy
Duson
Egan
Elton

Erath
Evangeline
Franklin
Garden City
Gueydan
Henderson
Iota
Iowa
Jeanerette
Jennings
Kaplan
Lafayette
Lake Arthur
Lake Charles

Loreauville
Mermentau
Morgan City
New Iberia
Parks
Patterson
Rayne
Roanoke
Scott
St. Martinville
Sulphur
Vinton
Welsh
Westlake

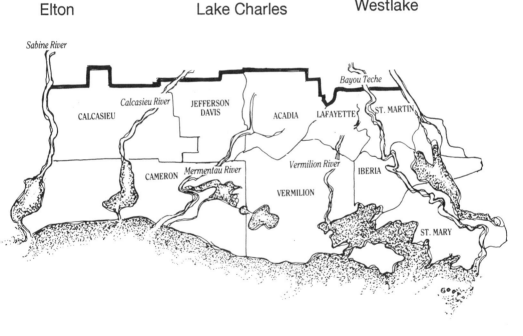

GULF OF MEXICO

Sunday Delight

SERVES 10-12

1 box yellow cake mix
3 eggs
1 1/3 cups milk
1/2 cup oil
20 oz. crushed pineapple
2 cups sugar
12 oz. Cool Whip
9 oz. cream cheese

1 small box instant vanilla
    pudding
2 cups milk
3 medium ripe bananas
1/2 cup chopped nuts
1/2 cup coconut
1/2 cup chopped maraschino
    cherries

Grease and flour a 9" X 13" cake pan. Mix together cake mix, 3 eggs, 1 1/3 cup milk and 1/2 cup oil. Beat at medium speed for two minutes. Bake at 350 degrees for 32 minutes. Remove cake from the oven and poke holes in the cake with the end of a wooden spoon. Heat 20 oz. crushed pineapple (drained) with 2 cups of sugar until the mixture starts to boil. Pour this mixture over the warm cake. Set the cake aside until it is completely cooled. Then mix 9 oz. cream cheese (softened) with small box of vanilla pudding and 2 cups cold milk. Pour over cake and refrigerate until pudding becomes firm. Slice bananas over entire cake and spread Cool Whip over the bananas. Sprinkle coconut, cherries, and nuts on top of the Cool Whip.

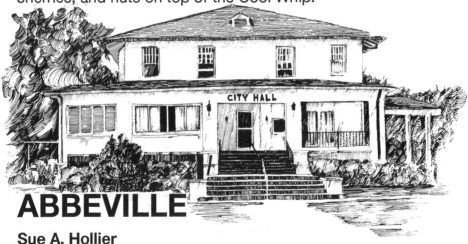

CITY HALL

ABBEVILLE

Sue A. Hollier
VERMILLION PARISH

Cherry Crisp

SERVES 10-12

1 can cherry pie filling
1/4 cup oleo
1 1/2 cups sugar, divided
1 cup flour
1 tsp. baking powder
1/2 tsp. salt
1/2 cup milk
1 tbsp. cornstarch
1/4 tsp. nutmeg
1 cup boiling water

Place cherry pie filling in 8" square pan. Cream butter and 1/2 cup sugar. Combine flour, baking powder and salt. Add to cream mixture with milk. Spoon mixture over fruit. Sift 1 cup sugar, cornstarch and nutmeg. Sprinkle over batter. Pour hot water over top. Bake at 350 degrees for 60 minutes.

AMELIA

Gladys Tabor
ST. MARY PARISH

Watermelon Cake

SERVES 12

1 box white cake mix
1 (3 oz.) package fruit gelatin mix
1 cup watermelon pieces
1 tbsp. plain flour
3/4 cup Wesson oil
4 eggs
ICING:
1 stick margarine, room temperature
1 cup watermelon pieces
1 box powdered sugar

Place cake mix in a large mixing bowl. Sprinkle flour over cake mix. Add gelatin, oil and watermelon. Mix thoroughly with electric mixer, adding eggs one at a time. Pour batter into 2 greased and floured round cake pans or one 9" X 13" pan and bake at 325 degrees until a toothpick inserted into cake comes out clean. ICING: Place margarine in a bowl, add sugar and watermelon. Blend well and spread over cake. All of watermelon may not be needed so add 1/3 cup at a time to obtain desired consistency.

BALDWIN

Lorraine Boudreaux
ST. MARY PARISH

Butter Chewy Squares

SERVES 12

1 box Duncan Hines butter cake mix
1 egg
1 block butter
1 (8 oz.) package cream cheese
1 box powdered sugar
1 cup coconut, optional
1 tsp. vanilla
2 eggs

Mix together the first three ingredients and press into a buttered baking pan. Mix remaining ingredients and pour over cake mixture. Bake at 350 degrees about 45 minutes. When cake cools cut into squares. Sometimes I leave the coconut out and mix in a cup of chopped pecans into cake layer.

BERWICK

Glynda Giroir Lasseigne

ST. MARY PARISH

Peggy's Peaches And Cobbler

SERVES 6-8

1 cup biscuit mix
2 eggs
1 1/2 cups sugar
2 tbsp. butter or margarine
2 tbsp. milk
1/2 cup cream sherry
3 cups sliced peaches, fresh or canned

Beat together eggs, 1 cup of sugar, add butter and milk. Add flour mixture and mix well. Pour into greased 9" square pan. Simmer sherry and remaining 1/2 cup of sugar together for 3 to 4 minutes. Add peaches. Pour hot peach mixture over batter in pan. Bake in moderately hot oven (375 degrees) for 30 minutes. Serve warm with a dollop of whipped cream or vanilla ice cream. Also good served cold. Quick and easy and delicious! Double recipe because it goes fast!

BREAUX BRIDGE

Peggy Lovell/Genevieve Baker
ST. MARTIN PARISH

Sad Cake

SERVES 8

1 box light brown sugar
3 eggs
2 cups biscuit mix
1 tsp. vanilla
1 cup pecans
1/2 cup chocolate chips
1/4 stick butter

Combine brown sugar, eggs and vanilla. Mix well. Add a cup of biscuit mix, a little of the melted butter, pecans and chocolate chips. Continue until all ingredients are used. *Note batter will be hard to stir. Do not use a blender. Spray bottom of 9" X 12" pan with Baker's Joy spray. Spread batter in pan. Bake at 375 degrees for 30 minutes or until done.

CAMERON

Kimberly Guilbeau
CAMERON PARISH

Sheath Cake

SERVES 8-10

2 cups sugar
2 cups flour
1 stick oleo
1/2 cup shortening
4 tbsp. cocoa
1 cup water
1/2 cup buttermilk
2 eggs, slightly beaten
1 tsp. baking soda
1 tsp. vanilla

FROSTING:
1 stick oleo
4 tbsp. cocoa
6 tbsp. milk
1 box confectionery sugar
1 cup pecans
Vanilla

Mix together sugar and flour and put to the side. Mix in pot, oleo, shortening, cocoa and water and bring to a boil. Pour over dry ingredients (stir well). Add buttermilk, eggs, baking soda and vanilla. Pour into 9" X 13" greased pan and bake at 400 degrees for 20 minutes or until done. Start frosting 5 minutes before cake is done. Melt and bring to a boil, oleo, cocoa and milk. Remove from heat and add 1 box confectionery sugar, vanilla and pecans. Mix well, spread over cake as you remove it from the oven.

CENTERVILLE

Angie Prados
ST MARY PARISH

114

Fudge Sundae Pie

SERVES 6-8

1 cup evaporated milk
1 (6 oz.) semi-sweet chocolate morsels
1 cup miniature marshmallows
1/4 tsp. salt
Vanilla wafers
1 qt. vanilla ice cream
Pecans

Mix evaporated milk, chocolate morsels, marshmallows and salt in a saucepan. Stir over medium heat until chocolate morsels and marshmallows melt completely and mixture thickens. Remove from heat and cool to room temperature. Line bottom and sides of a 9" pie pan with vanilla wafers. Spoon half of 1 qt. of vanilla ice cream over the wafers. Cover with half of the chocolate mixture. Repeat with rest of the ice cream and chocolate mixture. Top with pecans and freeze.

CHURCH POINT

Marilyn Scott Vidrine
ACADIA PARISH

Orange Fruit Cake

SERVES 12

1 cup butter
2 cups sugar
4 eggs
1/2 cup buttermilk
3 1/2 cups flour
1 tsp. soda

2 tbsp. grated orange peel
1 cup pecans
1 (1/2 lb.) package dates, chopped
2 cups powdered sugar
1 cup orange juice
2 tbsp. grated orange peel

Cream butter, sugar, eggs and buttermilk. Add and mix flour and soda. Add orange peel, pecans and dates and mix well. Pour into cake pan and bake in slow oven at 300 degrees for 1 hour and 45 minutes. Mix together powdered sugar, orange juice and 2 tbsp. orange peel. Pour 1/2 of cream mixture onto cake in the pan. Let mixture soak into the cake. Take cake out of pan and slowly pour the rest of mixture over the cake using a spoon so mixture will soak into cake. Use a toothpick to punch holes in cake to let mixture get in better.

CROWLEY

Mrs William J. Leonards
ACADIA PARISH

Ice Box Cookies

SERVES 10-15

2 cups brown sugar
1 cup butter
3 1/2 cups flour
1 tsp. vanilla
2 eggs
1 tsp. baking soda
1 cup pecans, chopped

Cream butter and sugar, add eggs, work in flour and soda.
Add vanilla and pecans. Roll dough out on wax paper.
Form a roll the size of the cookies you want. Cover roll with
wax paper. Put roll in ice box over night. Slice and bake at
375 degrees until desired crispness.

DELCAMBRE

Debbie Comeaux
VERMILION PARISH

Toffee Squares

SERVES 8

1 cup shortening
1 cup brown sugar
1 egg
1 tsp. vanilla
2 cups sifted flour
1/2 tsp. salt
1 bag semi-sweet chocolate chips
1 cup nuts, finely chopped or ground

Cream shortening and add brown sugar, beat until light.
Add egg and blend thoroughly. Add vanilla, flour and salt.
Mix well. Spread batter on 10" X 15" pan, (cookie sheet).
Bake 20 minutes at 350 degrees. Spread at once with
chocolate chips. Put back in the oven to melt chips, then
spread with knife to form frosting. Sprinkle with nuts and
cut into squares. A double recipe will fill a large cookie tin
for Christmas. A single recipe will afford a family dessert.

DEQUINCY

Mrs. James "Linda" Hester
CALCASIEU PARISH

Big Batch Cookies

MAKES 100 COOKIES

4 cups white sugar
2 lbs. brown sugar
2 cups margarine
3 lbs. peanut butter (crunchy)
12 eggs
1 tbsp. vanilla
18 cups oatmeal
8 tsp. baking soda
1 lb. chocolate chips
1 lb. M & M's
2 cups pecans

Mix together first six ingredients. Add remaining five ingredients and mix. Place on cookie sheet and bake at 350 degrees for 15 to 20 minutes. Note: This makes 100 BIG cookies. Bake what you need and roll the rest of the dough in wax paper and freeze. Then have fresh baked cookies when company drops by.

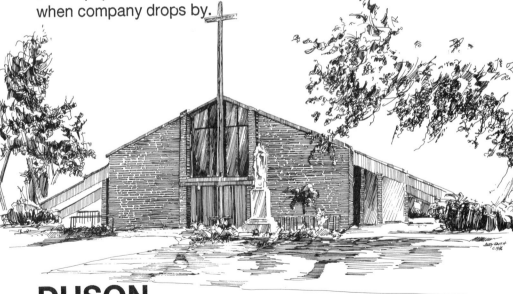

DUSON

Connie Hanks
LAFAYETTE PARISH

Almond Joy Cake

SERVES 8

1 box chocolate cake mix
1 1/2 cups evaporated milk, divided
2 1/2 cups sugar, divided
24 large marshmallows
1 (14 oz.) package coconut
1 stick margarine
1 (6 oz.) package chocolate chips
1 cup chopped almonds or pecans

Bake chocolate cake in a 9" X 13" pan according to package directions. Combine 1 cup evaporated milk and 1 cup sugar in saucepan then add marshmallows. Heat and stir until marshmallows are melted. Remove from heat and add coconut. Pour hot marshmallow mixture over warm prepared cake. After cake is completely cool, bring remaining 1/2 cup evaporated milk and 1 1/2 cups sugar and margarine to a boil and add chocolate chips and nuts. Pour over cooled cake. This is a very rich cake.

EGAN

Margaret Lejeune
ACADIA PARISH

Chocolate Chip Cake

SERVES 12

1 box Duncan Hines golden yellow butter cake mix
1 small box Jello instant chocolate pudding
1 cup cooking oil
1/4 cup water
4 eggs
1 (8 oz.) container sour cream
1 (6 oz.) package chocolate chips
1 cup pecans

Mix all ingredients together with mixer. Pour into greased and floured Bundt pan. Bake at 350 degrees for 1 hour and 15 minutes.

ELTON

Janet McCoy
JEFFERSON DAVIS PARISH

Ma Luke's Cream Pralines
SERVES 20

1 (1 lb.) box light brown sugar
1/8 tsp. salt
3/4 cup evaporated milk
1 tbsp. butter
2 cups pecan halves

Mix the brown sugar, salt, evaporated milk and butter in a 2 quart saucepan. Cook and stir over low heat until sugar is dissolved. Add pecans and cook over medium heat to a soft ball stage or to 234 degrees on candy thermometer, stirring constantly. Remove from heat and cool for 5 minutes. Stir rapidly until mixture is thickened. Drop rapidly from a tablespoon onto aluminum foil or a lightly greased baking sheet to form patties. Stir in several drops of hot water if candy becomes too stiff to handle easily. Let stand until cool and set.

ERATH

Terry Lancon
VERMILION PARISH

Date Loaf Candy

SERVES 20

3 cups sugar
1 cup dates, chopped
1 cup milk
1 cup nuts
Lump of butter
1 tsp. vanilla

Mix milk and sugar. Add chopped dates. Cook slowly until soft ball stage. Remove from fire and add butter. Beat until cool. Add vanilla and nuts. Wring out cloth in cold water. Pour on one side of cloth and roll up. Cool in refrigerator until firm. Slice.

EVANGELINE

Mabel Aycock
ACADIA PARISH

Carrot Cake

SERVES 8-10

2 cups flour
2 cups sugar
2 tsp. soda
2 tsp. cinnamon
1 tsp. salt
1 1/2 cups Crisco oil
4 eggs
3 cups carrots, grated

Mix and sift flour, sugar, soda, salt and cinnamon. Add Crisco oil. Add 1 egg at a time. Beat between each egg. Add carrots and pour into large pan. Bake 25 to 30 minutes at 350 degrees.

FRANKLIN

Geraldine L. Williams
ST. MARY PARISH

Pecan Date Pie

SERVES 8

1 (9") unbaked pie crust
3/4 cup butter
3/4 cup brown sugar
2 egg yolks
1/2 cup evaporated milk
2 egg whites
3/4 cup chopped pecans
1 cup dates
1/8 tsp. clove powder
1/4 tsp. cinnamon powder

Cream butter and sugar and beat until creamy. Add egg
yolks one at a time. Blend in milk, spices, pecans and
dates. Beat egg whites until stiff and fold into creamed
mixture. Pour into pie crust and spread evenly. Bake 40
minutes at 350 degrees. Serve with whipped cream on top.

GARDEN CITY

Sherry Luke
ST. MARY PARISH

Cherry Cheese Pie

SERVES 10

1 (9") graham cracker crumb crust
1 (8 oz.) package cream cheese, softened
1 can Eagle Brand sweetened condensed milk
1/3 cup lemon juice
1 can cherry pie filling
1 tsp. vanilla

In large mixing bowl, beat cheese until fluffy. Gradually beat
in Eagle Brand sweetened milk until smooth. Stir in lemon
juice and vanilla. Pour into prepared crust. Chill 3 hours.
Top with cherry pie filling. Refrigerate leftovers.

GUEYDAN

Jennifer Istre
VERMILION PARISH

Four Layer Crunch

SERVES 10

1 cup flour
1 stick margarine
1 cup chopped pecans
1 cup Cool Whip
1 cup powdered sugar
1 (8 oz.) container cream cheese
1 large box chocolate pudding
3 cups milk
1 tsp. vanilla
Cool Whip
Chopped pecans

Mix together first three ingredients and place in a 9" X 12" baking pan. Bake crust for 30 minutes in a 400 degree oven. Let cool. Blend the next three ingredients together to form layer two. Pour on top of crust. Combine and blend the next three ingredients for layer three. Top with Cool Whip and chopped pecans.

HENDERSON

Nellie Huval
ST. MARTIN PARISH

127

Sin Pie

SERVES 12

1 cup pecans
1 cup flour
1/2 cup brown sugar
3/4 stick margarine
FILLING:
1 1/4 sticks margarine
1 2/3 cups powdered sugar
1 (8 oz.) package semi-sweet chocolate chips
1/4 cup Amoretta liquor
2 eggs, beaten

Preheat oven to 350 degrees. Put pecans, flour and brown sugar into food processor and mix until powdery. Add melted margarine and mix. Pat mixture into a 10" pie pan. Bake at 350 degrees for 10 minutes.
FILLING: Cream butter and sugar. Melt chocolate chips and add to mix. Add liquor and beaten eggs. Pour into baked pie shell. Let set until firm in refrigerator. Garnish with whipped cream and pecans.

IOTA

Linda Lejeune
ACADIA PARISH

Muta's Jelly Roll

SERVES 10

3 eggs
1 1/2 cups sugar
6 tbsp. cold water
1 1/2 cups flour
1 1/2 tsp. baking soda
3/4 tsp. salt
Mayhaw Jelly

Separate eggs. Beat yolks until very thick and light. Add sugar gradually, beating well after each addition. Add water, mixing well. Sift together dry ingredients and add alternately with stiffly beaten egg whites. Line a 9" X 16" X 1" baking pan with waxed paper. Pour in batter and spread evenly. Bake in 375 degree oven for about 15 minutes until lightly browned. Turn out immediately onto damp cloth sprinkled with powdered sugar. Remove paper and trim off edges. Spread with slightly beaten jelly and roll while still warm. Wrap in damp cloth and when cooled, remove to plate and sprinkle with powdered sugar. Work quickly as cake will crack.

IOWA

Genevieve Franklin
CALCASIEU PARISH

Bakalava

SERVES 10

1 lb. Phyllo (filo)
1 lb. sweet butter (unsalted)
FILLING:
3 cups pecans, chopped
2/3 cup sugar
1/2 tsp. cinnamon
Juice of 1 orange

TOPPING:
1 cup sugar
1/2 cup water
2 tbsp. lemon juice
Juice of 1/2 orange
1/4 cup honey

(Handle filo carefully, keep covered.) Mix filling ingredients and set aside. Melt butter. Use pastry brush to oil bottom of cookie sheet. Place one sheet of filo in pan, brush with butter, place second sheet of filo in pan, brush with butter and spread 1/3 of filling over sheet. Add five more sheets of filo, brushing each one well with butter and add 1/3 of filling. Add five more sheets of filo and the remainder of filling. Cover with remaining sheets of filo, buttering each sheet. Oil top sheet with remaining butter. If filo is ragged looking, don't worry, just place all the edges in the pan. Before baking cut through the top layers only, into the traditional diamond shapes. Bake at 350 degrees for one hour. Begin boiling syrup during last 20 minutes of baking. Pour hot syrup over baklava. Let cool at room temperature, not in refrigerator.   Better after a day or two.

JEANERETTE

Gayle Clement
IBERIA PARISH

Phyllis's Buttermilk Pound Cake

SERVES 12

3 cups sugar
1 cup Crisco
6 eggs, separated
2 tsp. lemon extract
3 cups sifted flour
1/4 tsp. soda
1/2 tsp. salt
1 cup buttermilk

Blend sugar and Crisco in large bowl until light and fluffy. Add egg yolks, one at a time, beating well after each. Add lemon extract. Sift dry ingredients together. Add to first mixture alternately with buttermilk. Begin and end with dry ingredients. Beat egg whites until stiff. Fold carefully into batter. Pour into 10" greased and floured tube pan. Bake at 350 degrees for 1 hour and 10 minutes or until done.

JENNINGS

Janie Gary
JEFFERSON DAVIS PARISH

Brownie Trifle

SERVES 16-18

1 (19.8 oz.) package fudge brownie mix
1 (3.5 oz.) package instant chocolate mousse mix
8 (1.4 oz.) toffee flavored candy bars, crushed
1 (12 oz.) container Frozen whipped topping, thawed
Garnish: chocolate curls

Prepare brownie mix and bake according to package directions in a 13" X 9" X 2" pan. Let cool and crumble. Prepare chocolate mousse, omitting chilling. Place half of brownies in bottom of a 3 quart trifle dish. Top with half of the mousse, crushed candy bars and whipped topping. Repeat layers, ending with whipped topping. Garnish, if desired. Chill 8 hours. TIP: Bake brownies with pecans.

KAPLAN

Julia Trahan
VERMILION PARISH

Pear Cake

SERVES 12

1 1/2 cups salad oil
2 cups sugar
3 eggs
3 cups sifted all-purpose flour
1 tsp. salt
1 tsp. baking soda
1 tsp. cinnamon
1 tsp. vanilla
2 cups canned Bartlett pears, chopped (reserve juice)
1 cup chopped pecans

GLAZE:
1 tbsp. butter
1 1/2 cups powdered sugar
2-3 tbsp. pear juice

Combine oil, sugar and eggs. Beat well. Sift dry ingredients together and add to mixture. Add vanilla and fold in pears and pecans. Spoon into greased and floured Bundt pan. Bake at 325 degrees for 1 hour and 20 minutes. Cool in pan 20 minutes. Remove to rack to cool completely. Drizzle glaze over cake. GLAZE: Blend ingredients to make a smooth, slightly runny glaze.

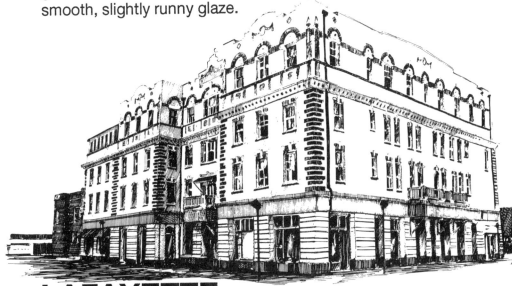

LAFAYETTE

Marilyn B. Hoffpauir/Marcee N. Bergeron
LAFAYETTE PARISH

Carry Cake

SERVES 10-12

1 box yellow cake mix
1 stick margarine
1 tbsp. water
1 egg
FILLING:
1 box powdered sugar
4 eggs
1 (8 oz.) package cream cheese

Mix the first 4 ingredients together in a 9"X 13" baking dish. Pat down on bottom of dish and sides to make crust. Mix the filling ingredients together in a bowl and pour over the crust. Bake at 325 degrees for 45 to 60 minutes.

LAKE ARTHUR

Katy Brunt
JEFFERSON DAVIS PARISH

134

Grandmother's Rice Pudding

SERVES 6

1 cup rice
2 cups boiling water
1 cup sugar
1/2 tsp. salt
1 qt. scalded milk
2 eggs, beaten
1 1/2 cups raisins
1 tsp. cinnamon

Boil rice in water. Add eggs, sugar, salt and cinnamon. Mix with scalded milk and raisins. Pour into greased baking dish. Bake at 300 degrees for 50 minutes, stirring occasionally.

LAKE CHARLES

Sallye LeBleu
CALCASIEU PARISH

Eve's Chocolate Drops

MAKES 125 CANDY BALLS

2 1/2 lbs. powdered sugar
2 cans coconut, Angle Flake
1 can condensed milk
1 3/4 blocks margarine
3 cups pecans, chopped fine
1 box semi-sweet chocolate
3/4 block paraffin wax

Mix first 5 ingredients together in a big mixing bowl. Then roll into balls, about 1 teaspoon at a time. Lay on waxed paper on cookie sheet and chill in icebox over night. Melt in double boiler, one box semi-sweet chocolate and 3/4 block paraffin wax. Keep low fire under chocolate. Put candy balls on toothpick and dip in chocolate, one by one, then lay on wax paper.

LOREAUVILLE

Eve Melancon
IBERIA PARISH

Creamy Caramel-Pecan Rolls

MAKES 20-24 ROLLS

1 1/4 cups sifted powdered sugar
1/2 cup whipping cream
1 cup coarsely chopped pecans
2 (14 oz.) loaves frozen sweet
   or white bread dough, thawed
3 tbsp. margarine, melted
1/2 cup packed brown sugar
1 tbsp. ground cinnamon
3/4 cup light or dark raisins

For Topping: In a small mixing bowl stir together powdered sugar and whipping cream. Divide evenly between two 9" X 1 1/2" round baking pans. Sprinkle pecans over sugar mixture. On a lightly floured surface, roll each loaf of dough into a 12" X 8" rectangle. Brush with melted margarine. In a small mixing bowl stir together brown sugar and cinnamon, sprinkle over dough. Top with raisins. Roll up rectangles, jelly roll style, starting from a long side. Pinch to seal. Cut each into 10 to 12 slices. Place rolls, cut side down, atop mixture. Cover with a towel. Let rise in a warm place until nearly double, about 30 minutes. Bake rolls, uncovered, in a 375 degree oven until golden, allowing up to 25 minutes for unchilled rolls. If necessary, cover rolls with foil the last 10 minutes to prevent overbrowning.
Cool in pans 5 minutes on wire rack.
Invert into a serving platter.
Serve warm.

MERMENTAU

Juanita Richard
ACADIA PARISH

No Roll Cherry Pie

SERVES 8

1/2 cup butter
1 tbsp. sugar
1 cup all-purpose flour
1 can (1 lb. 5 oz.) cherry filling
1 egg
1/2 cup sugar
1/4 cup flour
1/4 cup milk

In saucepan, melt butter with sugar over low heat. Add flour and stir until mixture forms a ball. Press into bottom and sides of 9 in. pie pan. Add cherry filling. Spoon over filling. To prepare topping: Beat egg with sugar. Blend in flour and milk until smooth. This mixture will be runny. Bake at 350 degrees for 50 to 60 minutes, until crust is golden brown.

MORGAN CITY

Marilyn Gautreaux
ST. MARY PARISH

Caramel Rice Pudding

SERVES 4

2 tbsp. seedless raisins
2 1/2 tbsp. rum, divided
1 cup Konriko brand
   Wild Pecan Rice, cooked
1 tbsp. orange peel, sliced
1/2 vanilla bean

1/8 tsp. salt
1 1/2 cups milk
1/4 cup heavy cream
1/3 cup + 2 tbsp. sugar, divided
2 egg yolks, beaten
2/3 cup apricot preserves, strained

Soak raisins in 2 tbsp. rum. Combine rice, orange peel, vanilla bean, salt and milk in 2 qt. saucepan. Cook, stirring over medium heat, until thick and creamy, about 20 to 25 minutes. Add cream and cook an additional 2 minutes. Discard vanilla bean and orange peel. Stir 2 tbsp. sugar, raisins and eggs into rice mixture and set aside. Heat remaining 1/3 cup of sugar and 1/3 cup of water in small saucepan until dissolved, boil without stirring, until syrup is a deep golden caramel color. Remove from heat and pour into 4 greased individual oven-proof molds. Pour rice mixture over caramel. Place molds in pan half filled with hot water; cover with foil and bake at 350 degrees for 1 to 1 1/4 hours, or until custard sets. Combine preserves and 1/4 cup water in small pan, heat gently. Stir in remaining 1/2 tbsp of rum. To serve, unmold pudding on plate, spoon sauce around pudding.

NEW IBERIA

Sandra Davis/ Konriko Conrad Rice Mill
IBERIA PARISH

Heavenly Hash Fudge Cake

SERVES 18

1 stick butter or margarine
1 block unsweetened chocolate,
  (baking chocolate squares)
1 cup sugar
2 eggs
1 cup flour
1 tsp. baking powder
1 cup pecans

1 tsp. vanilla
1/4 tsp. salt
Miniature marshmallows
ICING:
1 stick butter
1 block chocolate
1 box powdered sugar
1/4 cup canned milk

Melt together butter and chocolate. Add sugar, flour, baking powder, eggs, vanilla, salt and pecans. Beat well by hand. Pour into greased and floured 9" X 12" cake pan. Bake at 300 degrees for 35 minutes. Remove from oven and cover with miniature marshmallows immediately while still hot. Pour icing over marshmallows. ICING: Melt butter and chocolate. Beat in 3/4 box powdered sugar and milk. Mix well and cover cake.

PARKS

Leila Babin
ST. MARTIN PARISH

German Chocolate Upside-Down Cake

SERVES 10-12

1 box German chocolate cake mix
1 cup pecans, chopped
1 (8 oz.) package cream cheese, softened
1 stick butter, softened
1 box confectioners sugar
1 1/2 cups coconut

Pre-heat oven to 350 degrees. Grease a 9" X 13" cake pan. Prepare cake as directed on package. Stir in nuts and pour batter into pan. Blend cream cheese and butter. Add confectioners sugar and coconut. Drop by teaspoonsful on top of raw cake batter (mixture is very thick) until coconut mixture is all used up. Bake for 45 to 50 minutes. The cake batter rises and the coconut-cream cheese mixture settles to the bottom. Serve by spooning out portions. Delicious, moist cheesecake-like dessert.

PATTERSON

Mrs. Theda Cutrera
ST. MARY PARISH

Fig Cookies
MAKES 2 1/2 DOZEN

3 cups flour
2 cups sugar
1 stick butter
3 eggs
2 cups figs

Mix flour and sugar together. Melt butter and beat 3 eggs and add all together. Add 2 cups figs and mix well. Drop by teaspoonful on cookie sheet. Bake at 350 degrees for 15 minutes or until light brown. Makes about 2 1/2 dozen cookies.

RAYNE

Mary Lou Doucet
ACADIA PARISH

Walnut Caramels

MAKES 10 DOZEN

1 (14 oz.) can condensed milk
1 can light corn syrup
1/8 tsp. salt
2 tbsp. butter or margarine
1 tsp. vanilla
1/2 cup finely chopped walnuts

Line the bottom and two sides of 8" X 8" X 2" baking pan with aluminum foil. Butter bottom of foil. Heat milk, corn syrup and salt to boiling in heavy 1 1/2 qt. saucepan over medium heat stirring constantly. Cook over medium heat stirring frequently until candy thermometer registers 245 degrees or until a small amount of mixture dropped into cold water forms a ball. Stir in butter, vanilla and walnuts. Immediately spread in pan. Cool. Cut into 1" X 1/2" pieces. Makes about 10 dozen caramels.

ROANOKE

Ann Brown
JEFFERSON DAVIS PARISH

Peaches And Cream Cake

SERVES 12

3/4 cup all-purpose flour
1 tsp. baking powder
1/2 tsp. salt
1 (3 1/2 oz.) package vanilla pudding, not instant
3 tbsp. butter or margarine, softened
1 egg
1/2 cup milk
1 (15 oz.) can sliced peaches
1 (8 oz.) package Philadelphia cream cheese
1/2 cup sugar
1 tbsp. sugar and cinnamon

Combine first 7 ingredients in a deep bowl and beat for 2
minutes. Pour in greased 9" round glass pan. Open can of
peaches. Drain well and reserve 3 tbsp. of juice. Arrange
peaches in batter, at least 1 to 1 1/2 inches away from
edge. Soften cream cheese with 1/2 cup sugar and reserved juice. Spoon over fruit and away from edge.
Sprinkle sugar and cinnamon on top and bake
at 350 degrees for 30 minutes.

SCOTT

Dianne Robichaux
LAFAYETTE PARISH

"Gateau Sirop"
English Translation "Syrup Cake"

SERVES 20-24

1 1/2 cups white sugar
1 cup salad oil
1 cup syrup (Steens)
1 cup boiling water
2 tsp. soda
1 tsp. ginger
1/2 tsp. cloves
1/2 tsp. cinnamon
2 1/2 cups flour
2 eggs
Pinch of salt

Combine ingredients in order given, mixing soda with boiling water. Add rest of ingredients. Pour into 8" X 13" pan, (greased). Bake at 350 degrees for 40 minutes. Let cool and cut into squares.

ST. MARTINVILLE

Alita V. Sieber
ST. MARTIN PARISH

145

Strawberries Romanoff

SERVES 10-12

1 qt. sour cream
2 cups light brown sugar
Dash of nutmeg
Dash of cinnamon
1 tbsp. rum flavoring

Thoroughly mix all ingredients and serve over strawberries.
Optional: Serve with pound cake or butter cookies.

SULPHUR

Dale Salter
CALCASIEU PARISH

Ebony And Ivory Cake

SERVES 12

1 3/4 cups unsifted flour
2 cups sugar
3/4 cup cocoa
1 1/2 tsp. baking soda
1 1/2 tsp. baking powder
1 tsp. salt
1 tsp. cinnamon, optional
2 eggs
1 cup milk

1/2 cup vegetable oil
2 tsp. vanilla
1 cup boiling water
FROSTING:
3 egg whites
3/4 cup sugar
6 tbsp. white Karo syrup
Pinch salt
1 tsp. vanilla

Combine dry ingredients in large bowl. Add eggs, milk, oil and vanilla. Beat 2 minutes at medium speed. Stir in boiling water. Pour into greased and floured 9" pans. Bake at 350 degrees for 30 minutes. FROSTING: Combine all frosting ingredients in top of double boiler except vanilla. Beat over boiling water until very stiff, (5 to 7 minutes). Add vanilla and mix well into frosting.

VINTON

Carolyn Slack
CALCASIEU PARISH

Dream Pie

SERVES 24

1 stick margarine, melted
1 cup flour
1/2 cup chopped pecans
1 (8 oz.) container cream cheese, soften
1 cup sugar
1/2 cup Cool Whip
1 package instant chocolate pudding
Cool Whip for topping

Prepare crust by mixing margarine, flour and pecans. Spread into a 9" X 12" baking pan. Bake for 20 minutes in a 350 degree oven. Cool. Mix together cream cheese, sugar and Cool Whip and spread on top of crust. Prepare the pudding according to package directions and spread on top of cream cheese mixture. Top with Cool Whip. Must be refrigerated.

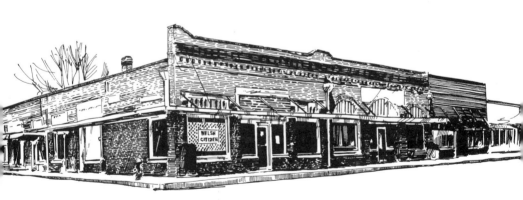

WELSH

Nancy Cormier
JEFFERSON DAVIS PARISH

Fruit Delight

SERVES 12-20

1 (21 oz.) can peach pie filling
1 (15.5 oz.) can crushed pineapple, drained
1 (11 oz.) can Mandarin oranges, drained
2 cartons frozen strawberries, thawed
3 bananas, sliced

Mix peach pie filling, pineapple, oranges and strawberries. Chill. Add sliced bananas just before serving. Serves 12. If I am expecting a large crowd, I just double or triple the recipe, adding a finely chopped apple, pineapple chunks, coconut, cherries, etc.

WESTLAKE

Marguerite Oliver
CALCASIEU PARISH

Central Section

Alexandria
Anacoco
Arnaudville
Basile
Bordelonville
Boyce
Bunkie
Cheneyville
Colfax
Cottonport
DeRidder
Dry Prong
Elizabeth
Eunice
Evans
Evergreen
Flatwoods
Georgetown
Grand Coteau
Hessmer

Hornbeck
Kinder
Krotz Springs
Lecompte
Leesville
Leonville
Loyd
Mamou
Marksville
Melville
Merryville
Montgomery
Moreauville
Oakdale
Oberlin

Opelousas
Palmetto
Pine Prairie
Pineville
Pitkin
Pollock
Port Barre
Rosepine
Simmesport
Simpson
Turkey Creek
Ville Platte
Washington

RED RIVER
GRANT
Black River
RAPIDES
VERNON
AVOYELLES
TEXAS
Atchafalaya River
BEAUREGARD
Sabine River
ALLEN
EVANGELINE
ST. LANDRY
Bayou Teche
Calcasieu River

Mrs. Kopacz's Fresh Apple Cake

SERVES 8-12

3 cups flour	3 cups chopped apples
1 tsp. salt	1 cup pecans, chopped
1 tsp. soda	Topping:
1 tsp. vanilla	1/2 stick butter
1 tsp. cinnamon	2 tsp. milk
1 1/4 cups oil	1/2 cup brown sugar
2 eggs	Sifted confectioners sugar
2 cups sugar	

Sift together the flour, salt and soda. Mix oil and vanilla into flour mixture. Beat 2 eggs well and gradually add sugar. Mix flour mixture and egg mixture together. Mix in apples and nuts. Pour into buttered tube or bundt pan. Bake at 350 degrees for 15 minutes then lower heat to 325 degrees and bake for 45 minutes. Let cool in pan. For topping, melt butter in sauce pan and stir in milk and brown sugar over the heat. Remove from heat and mix in enough confectioners sugar so that you have a thick glaze, not runny but not spreadable either. Pour topping over cooled cake.

ALEXANDRIA

Nancy P. Richey
RAPIDES PARISH

Mandarin Orange Cake

SERVES 10

1 box yellow cake mix
4 eggs
1/2 cup cooking oil
1 (12 oz.) container Cool Whip
1 small can Mandarin orange
   sections and juice
1 large can crushed pineapple
1 box vanilla instant pudding

Put yellow cake mix, eggs, cooking oil and orange sections in a bowl and beat for 3 minutes. Pour into greased and floured 8" X 13" pan. Bake at 350 degrees for 25-30 minutes. Mix remaining ingredients together and spread on cake.

ANACOCO

Pat Martin
VERNON PARISH

Double Peanut Butter Cookies

MAKES 2 DOZEN

1 1/2 cups sifted all-purpose flour
1/2 cup granulated sugar
1/2 tsp. soda
1/4 tsp. salt
1/2 cup shortening
1/2 cup creamy peanut butter
1/4 cup light corn syrup
1 tbsp. milk

Sift together dry ingredients. Cut in shortening and peanut butter until mixture resembles coarse meal. Blend in syrup and milk. Shape into 2" roll and chill. Slice 1/8 to 1/4 inch thick. Place half of the slices on ungreased cookie sheet. Spread each slice with 1/2 tsp. peanut butter. Cover with remaining slices. Seal edges with fork. Bake at 350 degrees for about 12 minutes. Cool slightly and remove from sheet.

ARNAUDVILLE

Stephanie Blanchard
ST. LANDRY PARISH

Betty's Cake

SERVES 15

1 3/4 cups sugar
2 1/4 cups flour
1 tsp. soda
1/2 tsp. baking powder
1/4 tsp. salt
3/4 cup butter Crisco
3 eggs
1 (20 oz.) can crushed pineapple and juice

ICING:
1 cup sugar
1 stick oleo
1 small can evaporated milk
1 cup coconut
1/2 cup chopped walnuts

Mix dry ingredients. Add remaining cake ingredients in order listed and beat for about 1 minute. Pour into greased 9" X 12" baking pan and bake 30 to 40 minutes. ICING: Mix sugar, oleo and evaporated milk in 2 quart pot. Add coconut and walnuts. Cook for 5 minutes, then pour on hot cake. Cool before cutting.

BASILE

Betty Aguillard
EVANGELINE PARISH

Aunt Emily's Cake

SERVES 12

1 box yellow cake mix
1/2 cup margarine
1 egg, slightly beaten
FILLING:
1 (8 oz.) cream cheese
2 eggs, beaten
1 box powdered sugar
1 tsp. vanilla

Mix the first three ingredients and put into a well greased
13" X 9" X 2" pan. Pat well. Mix filling ingredients and pour
into crust. Bake at 300 degrees for 1 hour.

BORDELONVILLE

Betsy Reason
AVOYELLES PARISH

Cream Cheese Delight

SERVES 12

1 package chocolate brownie mix
2 (8 oz.) packages cream cheese, softened
3/4 cup sugar
1 tbsp. vanilla
1 (8 oz.) container sour cream
2 cans cherry pie filling

Prepare brownie mix according to package directions. Bake and cool. Mix together cream cheese, sugar, vanilla and sour cream. Spread on top of brownies. Spread the 2 cans of cherry pie filling on top of the cream cheese mixture. Chill and serve.

BOYCE

Gorettia Knight
RAPIDES PARISH

Juicy Fruit Salad

SERVES 8-10

1 large apple
1 large orange
2 (10 oz.) jars cherries
3 jars of the juice from cherries
5 bananas
1 (16 oz.) can sliced peaches
1 (16 oz.) can crushed pineapple
2 cans condensed milk
2 cans evaporated milk

Cut apple, orange and cherries in small pieces. Slice bananas and add remaining ingredients. Chill and serve. It's great.

BUNKIE

Patrice V. Steele
AVOYELLES PARISH

Pat-A-Cake

SERVES 12-16

1 box yellow cake mix
1 box powdered sugar
3 eggs
1 (8 oz.) container cream cheese
1/2 cup chopped pecans
1 stick butter or oleo

Mix cake mix, butter, pecans and 1 egg together. Pat or press to the bottom and sides of a 9" X 13" baking pan. Mix together 2 eggs, softened cream cheese and powdered sugar. Pour over cake mixture. Bake 40-45 minutes in 350 degree oven. Cool about 3 hours before cutting.

CHENEYVILLE

Jennie T. Hoyt
RAPIDES PARISH

Lazy Daisy Oatmeal Cake

SERVES 16

1 1/4 cups boiling water
1 cup Quacker or
  Mother's Oats, uncooked
1/2 cup butter or
  margarine, softened
1 cup granulated sugar
1 cup firmly packed
  brown sugar
1 tsp. vanilla
2 eggs
1 1/2 cups sifted
  all-purpose flour
1 tsp. soda

1 tsp. salt
3/4 tsp. cinnamon
1/4 tsp. nutmeg
FROSTING:
1/4 cup butter or
  margarine, melted
1/2 cup firmly packed
  brown sugar
3 tbsp. Half & Half
1/3 cup chopped nutmeats
3/4 cup shredded or
  flaked coconut

Pour boiling water over oats, cover and let stand for 20 minutes. Beat butter until creamy. Gradually add sugars and beat until fluffy. Blend in vanilla and eggs. Add oat mixture and mix well. Sift together flour, soda, salt, cinnamon and nutmeg. Add to creamed mixture. Mix well. Pour batter into well greased and floured 9" square pan. Bake in preheated 350 degree oven for 50-55 minutes. Do not remove cake from pan. FROSTING: Combine all ingredients. Spread evenly over cake. Broil until frosting becomes bubbly. Cake may be served warm or cold.

COLFAX

Helen Sorrell
GRANT PARISH

Derby Pie

SERVES 8

1 (9") unbaked pie shell
1 (6 oz.) bag semi-sweet chocolate chips
6 tbsp. butter, melted
1 cup sugar
1/2 cup flour
2 eggs, slightly beaten
1 cup chopped pecans
1 tsp. vanilla

Spread bottom of pie shell with chocolate pieces. Combine butter, sugar and flour in separate bowl. Add eggs, one at a time to above mixture, mixing well. Stir in pecans and vanilla flavoring. Pour mixture over the chocolate chip pieces. Bake at 350 degrees for 50 to 60 minutes. Place pie shell on cookie sheet when baking.

COTTONPORT

Peggy Marchand
AVOYELLES PARISH

Vanilla Wafer Cake

SERVES 10-12

1 box vanilla wafers, crushed
6 eggs
1/2 cup milk
2 sticks oleo
2 cups sugar
2 cans coconut
1 cup pecans

Cream sugar and oleo and alternately add crushed wafers and milk. Add 1 egg at a time. Add coconut and pecans. Bake in angel food cake pan at 250 degrees for 2 hours. Icing is not necessary or you can use simple glaze.

DERIDDER

Anna Wiggins
BEAUREGARD PARISH

Pecan Bars

MAKES 40-45 BARS

1 cup brown sugar
1 cup granulated sugar
2 eggs
3/4 cup butter or margarine, melted
1 tsp. salt
1 1/4 cup flour
1 tsp. vanilla
1 cup pecans, chopped

Mix sugars and eggs. Blend in margarine. Add salt, flour, vanilla and nuts. Blend well. Bake at 350 degrees for 35 to 40 minutes in a lightly greased 9" X 13" pan. Cut bars while still warm. Makes 40 to 45 cookie bars. Store in a tightly sealed container.

DRY PRONG

Betty K. Reagan
GRANT PARISH

Fruit Cobbler

SERVES 4-6

1 stick margarine
1 cup flour, plain
1 cup sugar
1 tsp. salt
2 tsp. baking powder
1 cup milk
1 large can fruit

Melt margarine in pan. In bowl, mix together flour, sugar, salt, baking powder and milk. Pour on top of melted margarine. Drain juice and place fruit on top of batter. Bake at 400 degrees for 20 to 30 minutes or until brown.

ELIZABETH

Linda James
ALLEN PARISH

1-2-3 Cake with Pineapple Filling

SERVES 12

1 cup butter
2 cups sugar
3 cups flour
4 eggs, separated
1 cup milk
3 tsp. baking powder
1 tsp. vanilla
1/2 tsp. salt

FILLING:
1 stick margarine
1 box powdered sugar
1 (8 oz.) package cream cheese
1 (16 oz.) can crushed pineapple

Cream butter and sugar. Sift flour, baking powder and salt. Add to butter mixture, alternating with milk. Beat at medium speed for 2 minutes. Beat egg yolks until lemon colored and add to batter. Beat 1 minute. Beat egg whites until stiff and fold into batter with vanilla. Pour into three 9" greased and floured pans. Bake at 325 degrees for 30 minutes. Cool in pans before removing. FILLING: Cook pineapple until there is no more liquid. Add margarine, cream cheese and sugar, mixing well. Spread between layers and use as icing.

EUNICE

Charlotte Butler
ST. LANDRY PARISH

Buttermilk Coconut Pie

MAKES 2 PIES

1 1/2 cups sugar
2 tbsp. flour
1 stick margarine
4 eggs
1/2 cup buttermilk
1 tsp. vanilla
1 1/2 cups coconut
2 shallow 8" or 9" unbaked pie crusts

Mix first 6 ingredients together. Put 3/4 cup of coconut in each pie shell. Pour ingredients over the coconut, about 1/2". Bake at 325 degrees for 25 to 30 minutes.

EVANS

Alice Simmons
VERNON PARISH

Soft Chocolate Chip Cookies

MAKES 3 DOZEN

1/3 cup margarine
1/3 cup shortening
1/2 cup granulated sugar
1/2 cup brown sugar
1 egg
1 tsp. vanilla

1 3/4 cups flour
1/2 tsp. baking soda
1/2 tsp. salt
1/2 cup chopped pecans
1 (6 oz.) package
 chocolate chips

Heat oven to 375 degrees. In large bowl mix shortening, margarine, sugars, egg and vanilla thoroughly. Blend dry ingredients and stir into first mixture. Mix in nuts and chips. Drop by tablespoonsful 2" apart onto lightly greased baking sheet. Bake 7-9 minutes. Do not overbake! Cool slightly before removing from baking sheet. Makes about 3 dozen large, soft, yummy cookies.

EVERGREEN

Carol Heiman Miller
AVOYELLES PARISH

Dump Cake

SERVES 24

1 can blueberry pie filling
1 large can crushed pineapple
1 box white cake mix
1 cup chopped nuts
1 stick margarine, cut in small pieces

Butter a 9" X 12" pan. Place ingredients in pan in the order as listed above. (Do not mix the cake mix, use it dry.) Bake for 1 hour at 350 degrees.

FLATWOODS

Sue Vercher
RAPIDES PARISH

Best Ever Peanut Butter Cake

SERVES 12

1 Duncan Hines butter recipe cake mix
3 eggs
2/3 cup of water
1 stick oleo
1 cup of sugar
3/4 cup of water
1 tbsp. vanilla
1 heaping cup of peanut butter

Prepare cake mix using the eggs, water and oleo. Bake in a 13"x 9" cake pan as directed. Remove cake from oven but leave in pan and cool completely. When cake is cool, prepare icing. In a heavy sauce pan, combine sugar and water and bring to a hard boil. Boil for two minutes. Remove from heat and add vanilla and peanut butter. With an electric mixer beat on low speed until the icing begins to thicken and get a shiny look. Pour on cooled cake and spread. Let cake set until icing has completely cooled. Then serve and enjoy.

GEORGETOWN

Lou Ann Edwards
GRANT PARISH

Pistachio Pudding

SERVES 6

1 small box instant pistachio pudding
1 medium size can crushed pineapple (juice too)
1 cup miniature marshmallows
1 (9 oz.) container Cool Whip
1/2 cup pecans, chopped

Mix all ingredients together and refrigerate. Will keep for at least 1 week.

GRAND COTEAU

Cynthia Luquette
ST. LANDRY PARISH

Fruit-Filled Bread Pudding

SERVES 10

1 (16 oz.) French bread
1 can crushed pineapple and juice
12 Maraschino cherries, halved
1/4 cup butter
2 cups sugar
1 tbsp. vanilla
1 can sweetened condensed milk
3 bananas, mashed
1 cup raisins
6 egg yolks
2 cups milk

MERINGUE:
6 egg whites
6 1/2 tbsp. sugar
1 tsp. cream of tartar
1 drop vanilla

Preheat oven to 300 degrees. Slice French bread into small pieces and soak with milk. Add all other ingredients and stir. Mixture should be soupy. If not, add milk to thin. Bake one hour until top is browned and liquid is evaporated. MERINGUE: Beat egg whites on high speed until they form peaks. On low speed, add other ingredients. Spread over cooked pudding and bake until meringue is golden brown, about 3-5 minutes.

HESSMER

Fay Ducote Guillory
AVOYELLES PARISH

Chocolate Pies

SERVES 12

2 cups sugar
4 cups milk
1 cup plain flour
1 1/2 tsp. vanilla
4 tbsp. cocoa
4 egg yolks
1/2 cup chopped pecans

Mix sugar, flour and cocoa together. Add milk and eggs,
stir together. Stir over medium heat until it comes to a boil.
Add vanilla and pecans. Pour into two baked pie shells.
Cover with meringue and brown in oven. Makes two pies.

HORNBECK

Mary A. Moats
VERNON PARISH

Wishing Well Cake

SERVES 12

1 cup soft-type margarine
2 cups sugar
5 eggs
3-4 tsp. almond extract
1/2 tsp. salt
2 cups sifted all-purpose flour

Blend together margarine and sugar. Add eggs one at a time, beating well after each addition until light and fluffy. Stir in almond extract and salt. Gradually blend flour into creamed mixture. Turn into ungreased 10" tube pan. Bake in 325 degree oven for 1 hour and 20 minutes until cake tester inserted in cake comes out clean. Allow cake to cool a few minutes, then turn out and cool completely. If desired, invert cake and spread top with confectioners sugar glaze.

KINDER

Mrs. Lou Stagg
ALLEN PARISH

Eclair Cake

SERVES 16-20

CAKE:
1 (9 oz.) container
  Cool Whip
3 packages or 1 box
  graham crackers
3 small boxes
  vanilla pudding
4 1/2 cups milk

FROSTING:
6 heaping tbsp. cocoa
1 1/2 cups confectioners sugar
2 tbsp. oil
3 tbsp. soft margarine
3 tbsp. milk
2 tsp. light Karo syrup

Lightly grease bottom of 9" X 13" pan. Line pan with whole grahams. Mix pudding and milk until thick and blend in Cool Whip. Pour 1/2 of mixture over grahams. Put another layer of grahams on top of mixture. Pour rest of pudding mixture on top. Add another layer of grahams. Chill for 2-3 hours. Mix ingredients for frosting together and spread over cake. Refrigerate at least 8 hours before serving.

KROTZ SPRINGS

Tammy Wiltz
ST. LANDRY PARISH

"Gran's" Carrot Cake

SERVES 12-14

1 1/2 cups Wesson oil
2 cups sugar
4 whole eggs, well beaten
2 cups all-purpose flour
2 tsp. cinnamon
2 tsp. soda
2 tsp. baking powder
1 cup broken pecans
3 cups grated carrots

FILLING:
1 (8 oz.) package cream cheese
1 stick oleo
1 box powdered sugar
2 tsp. vanilla

Mix oil and sugar and beat well. Add eggs that have been beaten. Sift flour, cinnamon, soda and baking powder. Add nuts and mix with the above mixture. Add the grated carrots a small amount at a time. Bake in three 8" greased and floured pans about 30 minutes in a 350 degree oven. FILLING: Beat all ingredients well, spread between layers and on top of cake. This cake can be prepared ahead of time and frozen.

LECOMPTE

Maxine Buller
RAPIDES PARISH

Chocolate Lush

SERVES 12-15

1 cup flour
1/2 cup chopped pecans
1 stick margarine, softened
1 (8 oz.) package cream cheese
1 cup sugar
2 small packages chocolate instant pudding
1 large container Cool Whip
2 1/2 cups milk

Combine flour, pecans and margarine and press into 8" x 11 1/2" baking dish. Bake at 350 degrees for 10 minutes or until golden brown, then cool. Cream together sugar and cream cheese. Fold in 1 cup Cool Whip. Spread on cooled crust. Prepare chocolate pudding as directed on the package only using 2 1/2 cups milk. Spread on cream cheese mixture. Top with remaining Cool Whip and sprinkle with chopped nuts, if desired.

LEESVILLE

Voncil L. Stephens
VERNON PARISH

Baked Caramel Corn

MAKES 6 QUARTS

6 qts. popped corn
2 cups light brown sugar
2 sticks margarine
1/2 cup white Karo syrup
Pinch of cream of tartar
1 tsp. baking soda

Pop corn and set aside. Put brown sugar, margarine and cream of tartar in a saucepan and bring to a boil. Boil 5 minutes. Remove from heat and add soda. Stir. Put popped corn in large baking pan or roaster and pour hot syrup over it. Mix well to coat each kernel. Bake at 200 degrees for 1 hour, stirring every 15 minutes. Turn out of pan onto waxed paper. Note: You may add peanuts or pecans by putting the nuts into the syrup before pouring over the corn. Store in tightly covered containers or Ziploc bags.

LEONVILLE

Dolores Melancon
ST. LANDRY PARISH

Granny Fitzgerald's Cheese Cake

SERVES 8

2 (8 oz.) boxes cream cheese
3/4 cup sugar
3 eggs
1 tsp. vanilla
1 graham cracker crust

1 cup sour cream
1/2 tsp. almond extract
1/2 cup sugar

Mix together cream cheese, eggs and sugar until smooth and creamy. Add vanilla. Pour into graham cracker crust. Bake at 325 degrees for 25 minutes. Cool 20 minutes. Mix sour cream, sugar and almond extract together. Pour over cake and bake 10 minutes longer.

LOYD

Ann Fitzgerald
RAPIDES PARISH

Mississippi Mud Pie

SERVES 10-12

1 cup flour
1 stick butter, room temperature
1 cup pecans, chopped
1 (8 oz.) package cream cheese, room temperature
2 cups powdered sugar
1 (10 oz.) container Cool Whip
1 large box chocolate pudding
9" X 13" glass baking dish

Mix butter and flour together. Press firmly on bottom of baking dish. Sprinkle chopped pecans on top of butter and flour. Bake at 350 degrees for 20 minutes. Set aside and let cool. Mix cream cheese and powdered sugar then add 8 oz. of Cool Whip to mixture. Spread over baked and cooled crust. Prepare pudding as directed on box and spread over cream cheese mixture. Spread the rest of the Cool Whip over the pudding in a sweeping motion. Garnish top with chopped pecans if desired.

MAMOU

Edwina Chapman
EVANGELINE PARISH

Can't Fail Caramels
MAKES 1 1/4 POUNDS

2 cups sugar
1 cup firmly packed brown sugar
1 cup light corn syrup
1 cup heavy cream
1 cup milk
1 cup butter or margarine
4 tsp. vanilla extract

Combine sugars, corn syrup, cream, milk and butter or margarine. Cook slowly, stirring constantly to 248 degrees. (or when a small quantity dropped in cold water forms a firm ball) Remove from heat and add vanilla extract. Pour into greased 8" X 8" X 2" pan. Cool. When firm, turn out onto a board and cut into squares. Wrap each square in waxed paper.

MARKSVILLE

Justine Harris
AVOYELLES PARISH

Murl's Quick Lemonade Pie
SERVES 12

2 baked pie crusts
1 small can frozen lemonade
1 can condensed milk
1 (12 oz.) container Cool Whip

Thaw lemonade, then mix lemonade, condensed milk and
Cool Whip. Blend well. Fill both crusts and place in refrigerator to set.

MELVILLE

Murline Murray
ST. LANDRY PARISH

Fruit Cake Cookies

SERVES 20

1 (8 oz.) package candied pineapple
1 (8 oz.) package candied red cherries
1 (8 oz.) package candied green cherries
1 (8 oz.) box raisins
1 (8 oz.) package dates
1 can Eagle Brand milk
1 (8 oz.) package gum drop candy
1 box fruit cake mix
1 (8 oz.) bag pecans
1 (8 oz.) bag walnuts
1 (8 oz.) bag almonds
Vanilla wafers
Graham crackers

Chop all ingredients and mix. Crush vanilla wafers and graham crackers and add to candied fruits and mix well making sure all are coated well with cookie crumbs. Add enough Eagle Brand milk to mixture to make all ingredients stick together. Drop on cookie sheet by teaspoon and bake in 350 degree oven for 5 to 8 minutes. Just enough to melt mix together. Do not brown.

MERRYVILLE

Dorothy Williamson
BEAUREGARD PARISH

Chocolate Nut Crunch

SERVES 4

2 cups vanilla wafer crumbs
1 cup chopped nuts
1/2 cup butter or margarine
1 cup powdered sugar
3 egg yolks, well beaten
1 1/2 squares unsweetened chocolate, melted
1/2 tsp. vanilla
3 egg whites, stiffly beaten
Whipped cream and maraschino cherries for garnish

Combine 1/2 of crumbs and nuts and line the bottom of a 9" pan. Cream butter and sugar, add egg yolks, melted chocolate and vanilla. Mix well. Fold in stiffly beaten egg whites, gently. Pour mixture on top of crumbs, then sprinkle remaining 1/2 of crumbs and nut mixture on top. Place in refrigerator until chilled. Cut into squares and serve. Top with whipped cream and a cherry. Can be made the day before.

MONTGOMERY

Joan Curtis Boston
GRANT PARISH

Blackberry Pie

SERVES 8

2 cups sifted
  all-purpose flour
1 1/2 cups butter
1/2 tsp. salt
1 tsp. sugar
1 egg
1/3 cup milk

FILLING:
2 qts. blackberries
2 cups sugar
2 tbsp. butter
1 tsp. vanilla butter nut
  flavoring
1 tbsp. flour

CRUST: Sift together flour, salt and sugar. Cut butter into flour mixture. Beat egg, add milk to egg and mix with flour mixture. If not enough to make mixture hold together add water a little at a time. If too thin add flour a little at a time. Turn on floured board and roll out to fit a 9" pie pan. Keep enough dough to make a top crust. FILLING: Take a quart of fresh blackberries and put in a 2 quart sauce pan. Add sugar, butter and vanilla butter nut flavoring. Cook until berries are cooked. Add 1 tbsp. flour dissolved in water when berries are thick. Pour into crust. Put top crust and cut slits in top and bake in 350 degree oven until crust is golden brown.

MOREAUVILLE

Dorothy Johnson
AVOYELLES PARISH

Cherry Dream

SERVES 10

1 package of almonds, sliced
1 cup flour
1 stick butter
1 can Eagle Brand milk
1 tsp. vanilla extract
1 tsp. almond extract
1/4 cup lemon juice
1 large carton Cool Whip
3/4 can cherry pie filling

Blend flour and butter - press in 9" x 13 " dish. Sprinkle almonds thickly. Bake at 425 degrees for 15 or 20 minutes. Cool completely. Take Eagle Brand and lemon juice and both flavorings, fold in Cool Whip. Spread over cool crust. Set in refrigerator and let cool, spread pie filling over the pie. Um good!

OAKDALE

Alberta Luedecke
ALLEN PARISH

Ice Box Fruitcake

SERVES 10-12

1/2 lb. butter
1 bag large marshmallows
1 small bottle cherries
1 large box graham crackers
2 cups pecans
2 cups raisins

Melt butter and marshmallows in double boiler. Crumble graham crackers until fine. Combine all ingredients and mix well. Put wax paper in graham cracker box. Press all ingredients firmly in box and put in the refrigerator over night.

OBERLIN

Emily Adams
ALLEN PARISH

Grammy's Boston Cream Pie

SERVES 12

1/2 cup margarine
1 cup sugar
2 eggs, beaten
3/4 tsp. vanilla
2 cups flour
2 tsp. baking powder
1/2 tsp. salt
2/3 cup milk
FILLING:
1/3 cup sugar
3 tbsp. flour

1/4 tsp. salt
1 1/4 cups milk
1 egg, beaten
1 tbsp. margarine
1 tsp. vanilla
GLAZE:
2 tbsp. margarine
1 oz. unsweetened chocolate
1 cup powdered sugar
2 tbsp. boiling water

Cream together margarine, sugar, eggs and vanilla. Sift together dry ingredients and stir into mixture. Add milk and mix thoroughly. Bake at 350 degrees in 2 9" round cake pans. Cool. FILLING: In saucepan bring sugar, flour, salt and milk to a boil. Cook 2 minutes. Remove 1/4 of the hot mixture and add 1 beaten egg. Mix back into saucepan and bring just to a boil. Remove from heat. Stir in 1 tbsp. margarine and 1 tsp. vanilla. Chill. GLAZE: Melt together margarine and chocolate. Stir in powdered sugar and 2 tbsp. boiling water. To assemble split cool rounds into 2 layers. Spread cream filling between each, stacking 4 layers high. Top with chocolate glaze, letting it drizzle down sides.

OPELOUSAS

Gladys Boagni
ST. LANDRY PARISH

Pear Cobbler

SERVES 6-8

1 cup sugar
1 cup flour
1 tsp. baking powder
1/2 tsp. cinnamon
1 cup milk
2 cups pears, cooked or canned
1 stick margarine or butter

Set oven to 350 degrees. Place margarine in 13" X 9" pan and place in oven to melt. Measure dry ingredients in mixing bowl and blend well adding milk to mixture. Pour over melted margarine and drop pears in batter. Bake one hour. Serve warm with ice cream or Cool Whip.

PALMETTO

Eldine S. Budden
ST. LANDRY PARISH

Strawberry Pie

SERVES 8

FILLING:
- 1 (8 oz.) package of cream cheese
- 2 tbsp. lemon juice
- 1/2 cup sugar
- 1 tsp. grated lemon rind
- 2 tbsp. milk

GLAZE TOPPING:
- 1 pint strawberries
- 3/4 cup sugar
- 3 heaping tbsp. cornstarch
- 1/2 tsp. red food coloring
- 1 tbsp. lemon juice
- Pinch of salt
- Water

Prepare filling ingredients and spread into a 9" cooked pie shell. Then prepare topping. In a small sauce pan, mix the sugar, cornstarch and salt into a paste with 2 tbsp. of water. Put paste into 1 cup of boiling water and cook until thick and clear. Remove from fire and add lemon juice and coloring. Cool and fold strawberries into glaze. Pour over cream cheese filling. Keep refrigerated. Great Summer Dessert!!

PINE PRAIRIE

Brandy Dupre'
EVANGELINE PARISH

Best Ever Coconut Cake

SERVES 12-15

1 box Duncan Hines butter cake mix
1 small can Lopez cream of coconut
1 cup powdered sugar
1 cup sour cream
1 (9 oz.) bowl Cool Whip
1 tsp. vanilla
3 packages frozen coconut

Bake cake according to package directions in round cake pans. Cool. Slice and make 4 layers. Mix together sour cream filling; sugar, sour cream, Cool Whip and vanilla. Add 2 packages coconut. Pour cream of coconut over the cake layers, then put the sour cream filling on the layers until all layers are covered. Take 1 package of coconut and spread on cake. Put the cake in a sealed container and refrigerate for 3 days. A very moist cake.

PINEVILLE

Rosa Carter Crane
RAPIDES PARISH

Cane Syrup Cake

SERVES 8-10

1 cup cane syrup
1/2 cup butter
2 eggs
1/2 cup milk
1 tsp. vanilla
1 1/4 cups flour

Combine syrup, butter and vanilla. Beat eggs with milk.
Mix together all ingredients. Pour into well greased pan.
Bake 40-50 minutes in 350 degree oven.

PITKIN

Mrs. Ima Bass
VERNON PARISH

Fudge Pie

SERVES 6-8

1 stick margarine
1 square chocolate
1 cup sugar
1/4 cup flour
2 eggs, slightly beaten
1/2 cup nuts, optional
1/2 tsp. vanilla
1 baked pie shell

Melt margarine, chocolate and sugar together. Mix other ingredients and add to chocolate mixture. Pour into baked pie shell. Bake at 375 degrees until knife inserted into middle comes out clean. Good served warm with ice cream.

POLLOCK

Kathy Munger
GRANT PARISH

Pea Picking Cake

SERVES 8-10

1 box yellow cake mix
4 eggs
1/2 cup high grade salad oil
1 (11 oz.) can mandarin oranges and juice
1 (20 oz.) can crushed pineapple and juice
1 large package instant vanilla pudding
1/2 cup pecans, chopped
1 large container whipped topping

Into a large mixing bowl, put the cake mix, eggs and salad oil. Cut the mandarin oranges into small pieces and add along with the juice. Blend until moistened and then beat two minutes at medium speed. Grease and flour three 8" cake pans or spray with Pam. Bake in preheated oven at 350 degrees for 25 to 30 minutes. Cool at room temperature. FROSTING & FILLING: In a mixing bowl, put the crushed pineapple with all of the syrup and the large package of vanilla pudding. Mix together well. Add the chopped pecans and fold in the whipped topping. Spread between completely cooled layers and on top and sides of cake. Cover and store in refrigerator.

PORT BARRE

Cynthia Perron
ST. LANDRY PARISH

Cucuidate (Fig Filled Cookies)

MAKES SEVERAL DOZEN COOKIES

DOUGH:
1 stick butter or oleo
3/4 lb. Crisco shortening
3/4 lb. sugar
5 egg yolks
3 lb. plain flour
3 tbsp. baking powder
1 cup milk
3 tbsp. vanilla extract
1 tsp. almond extract
1 tsp. lemon extract
Pinch of salt
1/2 can frozen orange juice, thawed
FILLING:
1 qt. fig preserves
1 package dried figs
1 (6 oz.) package dried citron fruit
1 (6 oz.) package candied cherries
1 (15 oz.) box raisins
1 package dates, pitted
1 (4 oz.) package candied pineapple
1 small jar orange marmalade
1 pt. pear preserves
1 small jar apricot preserves
2 Hershey's almond bars
4 tbsp. cinnamon
3 tbsp. nutmeg
3 tbsp. allspice
1 1/2 tbsp. cloves
1 1/2 cups toasted pecans
1 1/2 cups toasted almonds
Honey or Karo syrup
ICING:
1 box powdered sugar
2 tbsp. Karo syrup
1 tsp. almond extract
5 egg whites

DOUGH: Cream oleo and Crisco; add sugar. Cream; add egg yolks and cream until light and creamy. Add all dry ingredients together; work into creamed mixture on pastry board. Work dough with hands, adding orange juice, extracts and milk. Add the milk a small amount at a time, using more or less of it as needed. Work dough until it is smooth. Filling: Grind all ingredients, except coarsely chop nuts. Stir in honey or Karo syrup to moisten and to hold together. Roll out dough on board into flat, thin strips 3" wide and 12" long. Place a roll of filling down the center of each strip. Seal edges together and roll back and forth lightly a few times. Cut in 1 to 2 inch pieces with sharp knife. Bake in 350 degree oven on ungreased cookie sheet about 20 minutes. Frost with icing, if desired. ICING: Whip 5 egg whites until stiff, then add sugar, Karo syrup and almond extract. Beat 5 to 10 minutes more. Put icing on each fig cookie individually, and ice lightly.

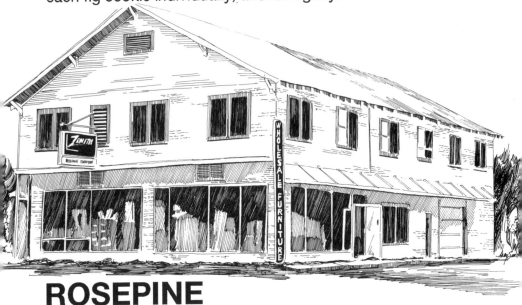

ROSEPINE

Jennie Sliman
VERNON PARISH

Moo Moo's Bread Pudding
SERVES 10-12

1 stick butter or margarine
1 1/2 cups sugar
3 eggs
1 can evaporated milk
1 1/2 cups water
1 apple, peeled and diced
1 tbsp. vanilla
Raisins, optional
8-10 slices toasted bread
   about 2 cups bread crumbs
Cinnamon
Nutmeg

Cream butter or margarine and sugar. Add eggs one at a time. Add the can of evaporated milk and water. Stir. (Looks like clabber) Add apple and vanilla. Pour into a glass 8" X 11 1/2" X 2" baking dish. Add toasted bread crumbs or toasted bread torn into pieces. Punch down. Sprinkle raisins and press down into mixture. Sift cinnamon and nutmeg on top. Bake 35-45 minutes at 350 degrees. A toothpick inserted in center should come out clean.

SIMMESPORT

Delores Rabalais
AVOYELLES PARISH

Aunt Sybil's Pineapple Dessert

SERVES 8

1/2 cup melted butter
1 cup crushed pineapple
3 eggs
1 1/2 cups sugar
1 cup chopped nuts
18 graham crackers

Beat eggs. Add sugar, pineapple, melted butter and nuts. Combine in double boiler. Place over boiling water and cook until it boils up once. Mixture will be thin, but thickens when cool. Roll graham crackers fine. Put 1/2 of graham crackers in bottom of 8" X 8" X 2" dish. Pour cooled mixture over crackers. Add remaining graham crackers on top of mixture. Chill.

SIMPSON

Bobbye Gordy
VERNON PARISH

French Chocolate Pie
SERVES 8

1/2 cup butter or margarine
3/4 cup sugar
2 squares Baker's unsweetened chocolate
2 eggs
2 cups Cool Whip
9" pie shell

Cream 1/2 cup butter with 3/4 cup sugar. Stir in 2 squares cooled melted chocolate. Add 2 eggs, one at a time, beating 5 minutes after each addition at high speed. Fold in 2 cups thawed Cool Whip. Pour into a cooled baked 9" pie shell. Chill until firm (about 2 hours) or freeze.

TURKEY CREEK

Melissa Roberts
EVANGELINE PARISH

Banana Pudding Supreme

SERVES 8-10

6 bananas
1/2 to 3/4 box vanilla wafers
2 cups very cold milk
1 large box instant vanilla pudding
1 can condensed milk
1 (8 oz.) carton whipped topping
1 tsp. vanilla or almond extract

Crumble vanilla wafers in bottom of large serving dish. (Reserve few crumbs for top). Slice bananas on top of wafers. Blend milk and pudding mix until thick then fold in condensed milk, whipped topping and extract. Pour over bananas and wafers. Top with reserved crumbs and refrigerate.

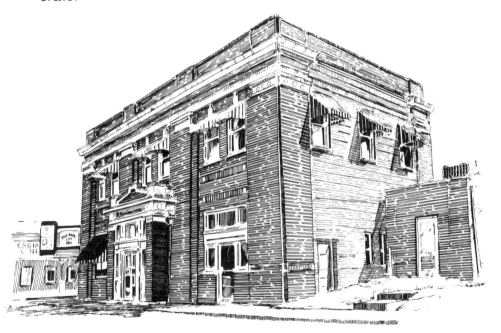

VILLE PLATTE

Sherrie Veillon
EVANGELINE PARISH

Sweet Pie Dough

MAKES 2 CRUSTS

3 2/3 cups flour
2 1/2 tsp. baking powder
1/2 tsp. salt
2/3 cup melted butter
1 1/2 cups sugar
2 eggs
4 tbsp. milk
2 tbsp. vanilla flavoring

Mix all ingredients together by hand. Roll out on floured
wax paper. Makes 2 9" pie crusts.

WASHINGTON

Darlene Lalonde
ST. LANDRY PARISH

Northwest Section

Ansley
Arcadia
Ashland
Athens
Belcher
Belmont
Bethany
Blanchard
Bossier City
Campti
Castor
Chatham
Choudrant
Clarence
Cloutierville
Converse
Cotton Valley
Coushatta
Cullen
Doyline
Dubach
Fisher
Gibsland
Gilliam
Grand Cane
Haughton
Haynesville
Heflin
Hodge
Homer
Hosston
Ida
Jamestown

Jonesboro
Keatchie
Logansport
Mansfield
Many
Marthaville
Minden
Mooringsport
Mt. Lebanon
Natchez
Natchitoches
Oil City
Plain Dealing
Pleasant Hill

Provencal
Quitman
Ringgold
Robeline
Rocky Mount
Rodessa
Ruston
Saline
Sarepta
Shongaloo
Shreveport
Simsboro
Springhill
Stanley
Summerfield
Vivian
Winnfield
Zwolle

Caramel Pie

SERVES 12-14

1 cup sugar, melted
1 cup sugar, loose
4 heaping tbsp. flour
5 eggs, separated
2 1/2 cups milk

Melt 1 cup sugar in heavy skillet. Mix flour and other cup of sugar. Beat egg yolks with milk. Mix all together in top of double boiler and cook until thick. Pour into 2 baked pie shells and top with meringue made with egg whites. Brown meringue.

ANSLEY

Jonnie Terry Lamkin
JACKSON PARISH

Bea's Lemon Pie

SERVES 8

1 cup sugar
3 tbsp. cornstarch
1/4 tsp. salt
2 cups milk
3 egg yolks, slightly beaten
1 stick butter
1 tsp. grated lemon rind
1/3 cup lemon juice

1 (9 in.) baked pastry shell
MERINGUE:
3 egg whites
1/4 tsp. salt
1 tsp. lemon juice
1/4 tsp. vanilla extract
6 tbsp. sugar

Combine sugar, cornstarch and salt in a saucepan, gradually add milk and stir until smooth. Cook over low heat for about 10 minutes, stirring constantly until smooth and thickened. Add a small amount of hot mixture into egg yolks, then gradually add egg yolks with the remaining hot mixture. Continue cooking and stirring constantly for about 5 minutes. Remove from heat. Add butter, lemon rind and lemon juice, blend thoroughly. Pour hot filling into baked pastry shell and cover with meringue, spreading all over. Bake at 350 degrees for 15 minutes or until lightly browned. MERINGUE: Combine egg white , salt, lemon juice and vanilla extract, beat until smooth. Add sugar gradually and continue beating until stiff. Add meringue onto pie filling. Cover completely.

ARCADIA

Beatrice Jefferson Hill
BIENVILLE PARISH

South Louisiana Pralines

SERVES 12-15

2 cups white sugar
2/3 cup brown sugar
1 stick oleo
3 tbsp. white Karo syrup
1 cup Pet milk
1 qt. broken pecans

Place all ingredients together in a medium size saucepan. Boil slowly to a soft ball stage. Take off stove and let cool for 10 minutes, then beat until it gets thick enough to drop by spoonfuls on waxed paper. When cool, pick up and put in a tightly covered tin or box. You may add 1 tsp. vanilla if wanted.

ASHLAND

Doris B. Vallery
NATCHITOCHES PARISH

Fresh Apple Coffee Cake

SERVES 15

1/2 cup butter or margarine, softened
2 cups sugar
4 eggs
2 cups all-purpose flour
2 tsp. baking powder
1/2 tsp. salt
5 cups apples, peeled and chopped
1 tsp. vanilla extract
1 1/2 tbsp. sugar
1/2 tsp. cinnamon

Beat butter at medium speed with an electric mixer. Gradually add 2 cups sugar. Beat well. Add eggs, one at a time, beat after each addition. Combine flour, baking powder and salt. Add to creamed mixture. Stir in apples and vanilla. Spoon batter into a greased and floured 13" X 9" X 2" pan. Combine 1 1/2 tbsp. sugar and cinnamon. Sprinkle over batter. Bake at 350 degrees for 45 minutes or until a wooden pick inserted in center comes clean.

ATHENS

Paula Liles
CLAIBORNE PARISH

Old Fashioned Apple Kuchen

SERVES 6

2 cups sifted flour	6-8 medium apples, Macintosh are best
2 tbsp. butter	1 cup sugar
1 tsp. salt	1 1/2 tsp. cinnamon
4 tsp. baking powder	1 1/2 tbsp. butter
1 cup milk	Lemon juice

Mix and sift the dry ingredients. Add butter and blend with pastry blender until mealy. Add milk gradually until a soft dough is formed. Place in a greased 8" X 10" cake pan. Peel and slice apples into eighths. Press them into dough so they are standing on the thin end of the slice (there should be about 4 solid rows of apples with no dough showing). Mix sugar and cinnamon together and sprinkle on the apples. Dot evenly with butter. Sprinkle very lightly with lemon juice. Bake at 350 degrees for about 1/2 hour or until dough is light brown and the apples are tender.

BELCHER

Linda L. Marino
CADDO PARISH

Fruit Pizza Pie

SERVES 8

2/3 cup margarine, softened
3/4 cup sugar
1 egg
1/2 tsp. vanilla
2 cups flour
1 (8 oz.) cream cheese
1/2 cup powdered sugar
1 tsp. lemon juice

Fruits you can use:
Bananas
Kiwis
Strawberries
Blueberries
Peaches
Pineapples
Cherries

In a bowl, beat together sugar and margarine until creamy.
Add egg and vanilla and beat well. Add flour and blend.
Press into pizza pan or chill and roll out and put on pan.
Bake at 350 degrees until golden. Mix cream cheese,
powdered sugar and lemon juice. When crust is cool,
spread this mixture over it. Let cool. Use three or four
types of fresh fruit or drained canned fruit. Arrange on pie in
wedges or mix. Drizzle lemon juice and powdered sugar
over pie.

BELMONT

Aleta Burr/Naomi Burk
SABINE PARISH

Peanut Patties

SERVES 12

2 cups sugar
1/2 cup Karo Syrup
2 cups raw or slightly cooked peanuts
  (I cook peanuts in oven for 15 or 20 minutes.)
1/2 cup water
1/2 tsp. vanilla

Mix all ingredients and cook to soft ball stage (235 to 240 degrees on candy thermometer). Remove from heat and let cool for 5 minutes. Add a few drops of red food coloring. Beat until mixture begins to thicken, then quickly drop onto greased sheet. Helps to have 2 persons to drop mixture on greased sheet.

BETHANY

Charlsie Alexander
CADDO PARISH

Strawberry Nut Bread

MAKES 6 LOAVES

2 sticks margarine, softened
1 1/2 cups sugar
1 tsp. vanilla
1/4 tsp. lemon extract
4 eggs
3 cups flour

1 tsp. salt
1 tsp. cream of tartar
1/2 tsp. baking soda
1 cup strawberry jam
1/2 cup sour cream
1 cup chopped pecans

Cream margarine and sugar. Add vanilla and lemon extract and beat until fluffy. Add eggs one at a time, beating well after each addition. Add dry ingredients; then add jam, sour cream and nuts. Mix well until all ingredients are combined. Pour batter into 6 greased and floured 3" X 5 1/2" loaf pans. Bake at 350 degrees for 30 to 35 minutes. Turn loaves out onto racks to cool. (This is delicious. It's good to use for gifts.)

BLANCHARD

JoAnn Powell
CADDO PARISH

Cracker Torte

SERVES 4-6

3 egg whites
1 tsp. cream of tartar
1 cup sugar
1 tsp. vanilla
1 cup pecans
16 saltine crackers, crumbled
2 tbsp. pineapple preserves
1/2 pt. whipping cream
1 package frozen coconut

Beat egg whites until dry. Add tartar, sugar and vanilla. Add pecans and crumbled crackers. Bake in a 9" X 9" ungreased pan for 20 minutes at 375 degrees. When cold, spread with 2 tbsp. of pineapple preserves and top with whipped cream. Sprinkle coconut over the torte. Chill. Can be frozen for several weeks.

BOSSIER CITY

Barbara Rowzee
BOSSIER PARISH

Betty's Tea Cakes

SERVES 12

1 cup oleo or butter
3 cups sugar
3 eggs
1/2 cup buttermilk
1 tsp. soda
1 tsp. flavoring
2-3 lbs. plain flour

Cream oleo or butter and sugar. Add eggs, one at a time until well mixed. Add flavoring. Sift flour and soda and add to mixture, alternating the buttermilk and stir until it is mixed where you can handle either by rolling on a floured board or pat with hands. Place on greased cookie sheets and bake at 450 degrees for 7 minutes or until brown. Makes 4 dozen.

CAMPTI

Virginia "Betty" Smith
NATCHITOCHES PARISH

Gold Angel Food Cake

SERVES 15-20

10 eggs
1 cup flour
3 tsp. cream of tartar
1 tsp. lemon extract
1 1/2 cups sugar
ICING:
1 cup sugar
1/4 cup lemon juice
1 egg
2 1/2 tsp. flour
1 tsp. butter

Sift flour once, measure then sift five more times. Separate the eggs. Beat yolks until light and creamy. Beat the whites until they foam then add cream of tartar and beat until they stand in peaks, gradually add the sugar, a small amount at a time. Add extract. Fold in flour and last the egg yolks. Bake in angel food cake pan. Put in cool oven, heat gradually. Bake 1 hour and 10 minutes at 350 degrees. ICING: Mix sugar and flour, add lemon juice and slightly beaten egg. Put butter in sauce pan. When melted add mixture and stir until boiling point is reached. Cool before spreading on cake.

CASTOR

Louise S. Havard
BIENVILLE PARISH

Sylvia's Yam Custard Pie

SERVES 12

1 1/2 cups sifted
  all-purpose flour
1/2 tsp. salt
1/2 cup shortening
3 tbsp. water
CUSTARD:
1 cup mashed
  sweet potatoes
1/3 cup brown sugar
3/4 tsp. cinnamon

3/4 tsp. ginger, optional
Dash salt
3/4 cup scalded milk
2 eggs, well beaten
TOPPING:
1/4 cup butter, softened
1/2 cup brown sugar
3/4 cup finely chopped
  pecans

Sift flour and salt into bowl. Take out 1/4 cup flour and mix with water to form a paste. Cut shortening into remaining flour until pieces are the size of small peas. Add paste to blended flour and shortening mixture. Mix with fork until dough comes together and can be shaped into a ball. Roll crust to 1/8" thickness and line a 9" pie pan. CUSTARD: Combine potatoes, sugar, spices, milk and eggs. Cool and fill pie shell. Bake at 375 degrees for 20 minutes. Sprinkle with topping. TOPPING: Combine ingredients, sprinkle on top of partially cooked pie and continue baking for an additional 25 minutes. Serve with whipped cream when cooled.

CHATHAM

Sylvia Honeycutt
JACKSON PARISH

Oreo Cookie Dessert

SERVES 25-30

1 package Oreo cookies, separated
1 stick butter or margarine
1 (8 oz.) cream cheese
1 cup powdered sugar
1/2 cup Cool Whip, large container
2 small packages instant chocolate pudding
3 cups milk

1ST LAYER: Crunch chocolate part of cookies in blender or food processor. Mix with melted butter, (save a small amount to sprinkle on top) and spread in long Pyrex baking dish. Put in refrigerator for 1 hour. 2ND LAYER: Mix middles for cookies (cream filling) with softened cream cheese. Add 1 cup powdered sugar and 1/2 cup Cool Whip. 3RD LAYER: Mix instant chocolate pudding with 3 cups milk. Top with large container of Cool Whip and sprinkle with remaining chocolate cookie crumbs.

CHOUDRANT

Meg Ball Thornton
LINCOLN PARISH

Two-Toned Cobbler

SERVES 8-10

1 can cherry pie filling
1 can apple pie filling
1 yellow or white cake mix
3/4 cup melted butter

In a large 3 quart baking dish, empty 1 can of cherry pie filling at one end and 1 can of apple pie filling at the other end. Top this with dry white or yellow cake mix. Melt butter and drizzle over the entire baking dish. Bake until done and fairly brown. Use temperature setting the same as for baking a cake on the cake mix box.

CLARENCE

Rose L. Manasco
NATCHITOCHES PARISH

217

Pauding Au Bon Camarade (Tipsy Squire)

SERVES 6-8

Leftover sponge cake
Brandy or Sherry Wine
Oeufs au Lait
  "Boiled Custard"

OEUFS AU LAIT:
1 qt. milk
4 eggs
1 tbsp. cornstarch or
  2 tbsp. rice flour
1/2 cup sugar
1 tsp. vanilla

Set milk to boil. Beat egg yolks with sugar until very light. Beat whites until stiff, fold into yolk mixture. Moisten cornstarch with a little cold milk and stir into boiling milk. Continue to stir until milk thickens. Then add egg mixture. Stir and cook for 1 minute. Remove from heat and add vanilla. Saturate cake with Brandy or Wine. Place in a deep bowl. Pour custard over it and serve very cold.

CLOUTIERVILLE

Amanda Chenault
NATCHITOCHES PARISH

"100" Sugar Cookies

SERVES 100

1 cup powdered sugar
1 cup granulated sugar
1 cup margarine, softened
1 cup vegetable oil
2 eggs
1 tsp. vanilla flavoring
1/2 tsp. almond flavoring
1 tsp. soda
1 tsp. cream of tartar
1 scant tsp. salt
4 1/4 cups all-purpose flour

Cream together the sugars, margarine, oil, eggs, flavorings, soda, cream of tartar and salt. Add the flour, one cup at a time. Beat well after each addition of flour. Roll dough into small balls and place on ungreased cookie sheets. Pat to flatten slightly. Sprinkle with colored sugar. Bake at 375 degrees until light golden brown on the edges, approximately 10 minutes.

CONVERSE

Cathy Singletary
SABINE PARISH

Oreo Cake

SERVES 12

1 package Oreos (35 or more)
1/4 cup butter or margarine
2 (8 oz.) packages cream cheese
1 (1 lb.) box powdered sugar
1 box instant milk chocolate pudding mix
1 3/4 cups milk
1 medium container Cool Whip

1st. layer: Using a food processor, mix 20 Oreo cookies with 1/4 cup butter. Blend until fine crumbs. Spread firmly on the bottom of a 9" X 13" baking dish. Bake at 350 degrees for 10 minutes. Cool. 2nd. layer: Mix 2 packages of cream cheese and 1 box of powdered sugar and spread on the first layer. 3rd. layer: Blend 15 oreos until fine crumbs. Spread over cream cheese layer. 4th layer: Mix 1 box instant milk chocolate pudding mix with 1 3/4 cups milk. Spread on top of Oreos. Chill until pudding layer is firm. Final layer: Spread Cool Whip on top of pudding. Chill for several hours before serving.

COTTON VALLEY

Rebecca Salley Holtzclaw
WEBSTER PARISH

Pumpkin Bread
SERVES 10

3 cups sugar
4 eggs
1 cup cooking oil
1 (#303) can pumpkin
3 1/3 cups flour
1 tsp. salt
2 tsp. soda
2 tsp. nutmeg
3 tsp. cinnamon
1 cup raisins or dates cut into small pieces
1 cup pecans
2/3 cup water

Mix all ingredients together . Pour into 4 (1lb.) coffee cans which have been greased and floured, filling each can only half full. Bake 1 hour or until done in a 325 degrees oven.

COUSHATTA
Rhonda W. Chamberlin
RED RIVER PARISH

221

Ugly Cake

SERVES 12

1 (8 oz.) package cream cheese
1 stick margarine
1 (16 oz.) box powdered sugar
1 box yellow pudding cake mix

Mix together cream cheese, margarine and powdered sugar until creamy and fluffy. Set aside. Prepare cake according to package directions. Set aside. Pour cream cheese mixture into sheet cake pan, 11" X 13". Spread evenly . Pour cake mix batter into sheet cake pan, on top of cream cheese mixture. Bake at 350 degrees or until cake is done. Turn out while still hot. Scrape all remaining mixture onto top of cake. Does not look real pretty, but is delicious.

CULLEN

Margaret Baldwin
WEBSTER PARISH

Banana Bundt Pan Cake

SERVES 20-22

3 cups flour
2 cups sugar
1 tsp. baking soda
1 tsp. salt
1 tsp. cinnamon
1 1/2 tsp. vanilla
3 unbeaten eggs
1 1/2 cups light cooking oil
2 cups mashed bananas
1 (8 oz.) can crushed pineapple, undrained
1 cup chopped nuts

Mix together, starting with flour, sugar and all other ingredients as listed, until well blended (by hand). Pour into a well greased and floured bundt pan and bake at 350 degrees for 1 hour and 20 minutes.

DOYLINE

Don Griffith
WEBSTER PARISH

Bacardi Rum Cake

SERVES 24

1 cup chopped pecans
  or walnuts
1 (18.5 oz.) package yellow
  cake mix
1 (3.75 oz.) package Jello
  vanilla instant pudding
4 eggs
1/2 cup cold water
1/2 cup Wesson oil

1/2 cup Bacardi
  dark rum (80 proof)
GLAZE:
1/4 lb. butter
1/4 cup water
1 cup granulated sugar
1/2 cup Bacardi
  dark rum (80 proof)

Make it with regular or pudding cake mix. Preheat oven to 325 degrees. Grease and flour 10" tube pan or 12 cup Bundt pan. If using yellow cake mix with pudding already in the mix; omit instant pudding. Use 3 eggs instead of 4 and 1/3 cup oil instead of 1/2 cup. Sprinkle nuts over bottom of pan. Mix all cake ingredients together. Pour batter over nuts. Bake 1 hour. Cool. Invert on serving plate. Use ice pick to punch all the way through cake so glaze will penetrate all through. Spoon and brush glaze evenly over top and sides. Allow cake to absorb glaze. Repeat until glaze is used up. GLAZE: Melt butter in saucepan. Stir in water and sugar. Boil 5 minutes, stirring constantly. Remove from heat. Stir in rum.

DUBACH

LaFon Colvin
LINCOLN PARISH

Glazed Blueberry Pie

SERVES 8

1 (3 oz.) package cream cheese
1 9" baked pastry shell
4 cups fresh blueberries
1/2 cup water
3/4 cup sugar
2 tbsp. cornstarch
2 tbsp. lemon juice

Soften cream cheese, spread in bottom of cooled pastry shell. Fill shell with 3 cups of blueberries. To remaining cup of berries add water and bring to a boil. Lower heat and simmer for 2 minutes. Strain and reserve 1/2 cup of juice. Combine sugar and cornstarch. Add reserved 1/2 cup of juice. Cook, stirring constantly until thick and clear. Add lemon juice after cooling slightly. Pour over berries in pastry shell. Chill 2 hours and serve with whipped cream.

FISHER

Melba Gillespie
SABINE PARISH

225

Louisiana Beauregard Yam Delight

SERVES 6

2 cups Louisiana Beauregard yams, cooked and mashed
3/4 cup sugar
3 eggs, beaten
1 tsp. lemon juice
3/4 stick margarine
1 tsp. salt
1 unbaked pie shell

Mix all ingredients together. Pour into unbaked pie shell. Bake for 10 minutes at 450 degrees, then turn oven down to 350 degrees and bake for 30 minutes. Test for doneness by inserting a toothpick in center.

GIBSLAND

Barbara Johnson
BIENVILLE PARISH

Buttermilk Cake

SERVES 12

1 cup butter
3 cups sugar
3 cups flour
6 eggs
1 cup buttermilk
3 tsp. vanilla flavoring
1/4 tsp. baking soda

Cream butter and sugar. Add eggs one at a time. Sift dry
ingredients together and add alternately with milk. Add
flavoring. Bake in a greased and floured tube cake pan.
Start in cold oven. Bake for 90 minutes at 300 degrees.

GILLIAM

Gail Moore
CADDO PARISH

Fruit and Sherbet Dessert

SERVES 8

4 oranges, peeled, seeded and sectioned
2 grapefruit, peeled, seeded and sectioned
1 (15 oz.) can pineapple chunks
1 pt. lemon or orange sherbet

Combine oranges, grapefruit and pineapple. Cover and chill. Spoon into sherbet glasses and top each with a small scoop of sherbet. Serve with cookies.

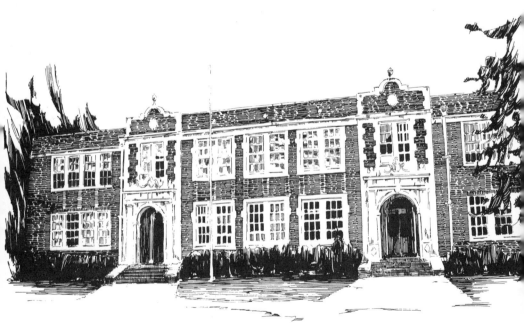

GRAND CANE

Martha Wilcox
DESOTO PARISH

Coconut Icebox Cake

SERVES 8-10

1 box yellow cake mix
1 can Creme de Coconut
1 can Eagle Brand milk
1 small container Cool Whip
1/2 can grated coconut

Bake cake as directed in a 9" X 13" pan. As cake cools, poke holes in the cake, using a fork or small round object. Mix Creme de Coconut and Eagle Brand milk in a bowl and pour over top of cake. Layer Cool Whip on top of cake. Sprinkle grated coconut on top. Refrigerate cake before serving.

HAUGHTON

Candy Murphy
BOSSIER PARISH

Date Nut Loaf

SERVES 8

4 cups sugar
1 large can Pet milk
3 tbsp. Karo syrup
1 tsp. vanilla
1 package chopped dates
1 stick oleo
1 qt. chopped pecans

Combine sugar, milk, Karo and oleo. When mixture is thoroughly blended and creamy, add dates. Cook over low heat until candy makes a soft ball. Remove from heat, add vanilla and beat with a spoon until mixture loses its glaze. Add pecans. Have a damp dish towel ready and pour candy out on it forming a long roll, roll up. When candy sets, unwrap and rewrap in waxed paper. Refrigerate, slice and serve. A Phillips family Christmas favorite.

HAYNESVILLE

Betty Phillips
CLAIBORNE PARISH

Italian Cream Cake

SERVES 12-15

1 stick oleo
1/2 cup Crisco
2 cups sugar
5 eggs
1 cup buttermilk
1 tsp. baking soda
2 cups flour

1 cup coconut
1 tsp. vanilla
FILLING:
1 (8 oz.) cream cheese
1 stick oleo
1 box powdered sugar
1 tsp. vanilla
1 cup nuts

Cream together oleo, Crisco and sugar. Add buttermilk, flour, soda, coconut and vanilla. Separate eggs and add yolks one at a time to batter. Beat egg whites until fluffy and fold into batter. Pour into 3 9" greased and floured cake pans. Bake at 350 degrees for 25 to 30 minutes. Allow to cool before adding filling. FILLING: Mix cream cheese, oleo, powdered sugar, vanilla and nuts. Spread between layers and top of cake.

HEFLIN

Effie H. Connell
WEBSTER PARISH

Blonde Brownies

SERVES 6-8

1 cup light brown sugar
1 cup plain flour
1 egg
1 stick butter or margarine
1 tsp. vanilla
1 tsp. baking powder
1 cup nuts
1/8 tsp. salt

Melt butter, add sugar. Stir in egg. Mix flour, salt and baking powder. Add to butter and egg mixture. Stir in vanilla flavoring and nuts. Bake at 350 degrees for 25 minutes. Do not overcook. Brownies are very chewy.

HODGE

Nelda Hollis
JACKSON PARISH

Lemon Cheesecake Bars

SERVES 12-15

1 package Duncan Hines lemon supreme cake mix
1 stick margarine
4 eggs
1 (8 oz.) package cream cheese
1 box powdered sugar
2 tbsp. lemon juice

Preheat oven to 350 degrees. Melt margarine in 13" X 9" X 2" cake pan. Swish around to get all sides of the pan coated. Pour melted margarine into cake mix in a bowl. Add 1 egg and blend together until mixture looks like cookie dough. Press it out into your cake pan. In a mixing bowl, beat remaining 3 eggs, powdered sugar, lemon juice and cream cheese. Pour over crust and bake for 45 minutes at 350 degrees.

HOMER

Betty Allen
CLAIBORNE PARISH

Peach Cobbler
SERVES 10-12

1 box yellow cake mix
2 cans sliced peaches with juice
1 stick oleo

Use Pyrex baking dish 13" X 9". Pour 2 cans sliced peaches in dish. Pour the cake mix over the peaches. Then cut the oleo in slices and put over the dry cake mix. Bake at 350 degrees for 50 to 60 minutes. When cobbler is half done (about 25 to 30 minutes) mash down crust and put back in oven and complete cooking.

HOSSTON

Louise Crowley
CADDO PARISH

Sweet Potato Casserole

SERVES 8

4 cups mashed sweet potatoes
1 cup sugar
1 stick butter
2 eggs, beaten
1 tbsp. vanilla
1/2 cup flour
TOPPING:
1 cup light brown sugar
1/2 cup flour
1/3 cup butter

Beat potatoes, sugar, butter, eggs, vanilla and flour together. Put in casserole dish. Mix together topping and
crumble onto the top of potato mixture. Bake at 350 degrees for 25 minutes.

IDA

Ann Chandler
CADDO PARISH

Egg Custard

SERVES 8

5 eggs, beaten
1 cup sugar
2 cups milk
1/2 stick oleo

Mix all ingredients together. Cook on top of stove until oleo
melts. Pour in partially cooked crust. Bake 5 minutes at
400 degrees and 5 minutes at 425 degrees. I use Pillsbury
Ready Crust.

JAMESTOWN

Loveey W. Guice
BIENVILLE PARISH

Pecan Pies (Ole Timey Recipe)

SERVES 16

2 cups sugar
6 eggs
1 cup white Karo syrup
1/2 stick oleo
1 tsp. vanilla
2 cups pecans, halves or chopped
2 unbaked pie shells

Makes 2 shallow dish pecan pies. Using two unbaked pie shells, put 1 cup pecans in each shell and set aside. Cream sugar and eggs in a sauce pan; add Karo syrup, vanilla and oleo. Cook just until mixture is blended and oleo is melted. Pour into pie shells and bake 45 minutes to 1 hour (until golden brown) at 300 degrees. Use 1 1/2 recipe for two deep dish pies.

JONESBORO

Mrs. Betty M. Savage
JACKSON PARISH

Cookie Crumble

SERVES 12-15

3/4 cup butter, melted
1 box German chocolate cake mix
1 cup pecans, chopped
1 cup semi-sweet chocolate chips
1 (14 oz.) can condensed milk
1 (12 oz.) package caramels

Mix cake mix, 3/4 can of milk, pecans and butter together. Spread 1/2 batter into a 9" X 13" greased and floured dish. Bake for 6 minutes at 350 degrees. Melt caramels with 1/4 can milk on stove top while half of batter cooks for 6 minutes. Sprinkle chocolate chips onto cooked batter. Spread caramels mixture on top of chips. Crumble remaining dough onto the caramel. Cook 15 to 20 minutes. Do not overcook. Enjoy.

KEATCHIE

Rene' Becnel Williams
DESOTO PARISH

Magic Cookie Bars

SERVES 8-10

1/2 cup margarine
1 1/2 cups graham cracker crumbs
1 (14 oz.) can Eagle Brand sweetened condensed milk
1 cup semi-sweet chocolate chips
1 (3 1/2 oz.) can flaked coconut
1 cup chopped nuts

Preheat oven to 350 degrees (325 degrees for glass dish).
Melt margarine in the oven in a 13" X 9" baking pan.
Sprinkle crumbs over margarine. Pour condensed milk over
crumbs. Top with remaining ingredients. Press down
firmly. Bake 25 to 30 minutes or until lightly browned. Cool.
Cut into bars. Store loosely covered at room temperature.

LOGANSPORT

Joyce Warren
DESOTO PARISH

Hot Peach Cream Pudding

SERVES 8

1 large can sliced peaches, drain and reserve juice
1 (8 oz.) package cream cheese
3/4 cup milk
3/4 cup flour
3/4 cup sugar
1 large package vanilla instant pudding mix
Cinnamon

Blend pudding and flour. Stir in milk and peach juice. Pour into 1/2 quart casserole dish that has been sprayed with Pam. Place peach slices on top. Soften cream cheese and beat sugar into it. Spoon dollops of cream cheese mixture onto top of peaches. Sprinkle with cinnamon. Bake 30-40 minutes at 350 degrees.

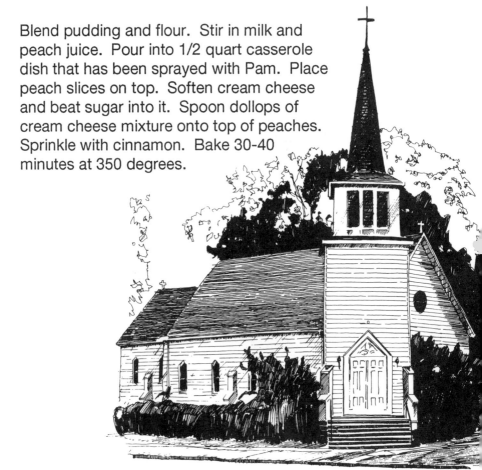

MANSFIELD

Syble Shoalmire
DESOTO PARISH

Ooey Gooey Butter Cake

SERVES 12

1 box yellow cake mix
2 eggs
1 stick oleo
1 (8 oz.) package cream cheese, softened
2 eggs
1 box powdered sugar

Preheat oven to 350 degrees. Grease pan, do not flour. Mix one box yellow cake mix with eggs and oleo. Spread this mixture in pan. Then mix cream cheese, 2 eggs and 1 box powdered sugar, less 4 tbsp. and spread on top of cake batter. Bake at 350 degrees for approximately 40 minutes until golden brown. Cake will look like a meringue and cannot be tested by toothpick or touch method. Sprinkle with remaining powdered sugar. Serve warm or cool.

MANY

Marilyn Nichols
SABINE PARISH

Fruit Filled Layered Angel Cake Dessert

SERVES 8

1 angel food cake
2 (3 1/2 oz.) boxes vanilla instant pudding
2 cups skim milk
1 (8 oz.) container Cool Whip
2 pt. strawberries, cut in half

Tear cake into 1" pieces. Prepare pudding as directed on package. Fold in 2 cups Cool Whip. Reserve remaining Cool Whip for garnish. Place layer of cake in a serving bowl. Top with a layer of pudding mixture, then a layer of strawberries. Repeat until all ingredients are used. Refrigerate at least 4 hours.

MARTHAVILLE

Brenda Youngblood
NATCHITOCHES PARISH

242

Pumpkin Pie Cake

SERVES 16

1 (30 oz.) can pumpkin pie mix
1 (13 oz.) can evaporated milk
4 eggs
1 box yellow cake mix
1 cup margarine
1 cup chopped pecans

Mix pumpkin pie mix with 1 can evaporated milk and 4 eggs. Pour mix into 9 1/2" X 12" X 3 1/2" pan. Sprinkle dry cake mix over top. Melt cup of margarine and pour over top of cake mix. Sprinkle 1 cup chopped pecans over top of cake. Bake 1 1/2 hours at 350 degrees.

MINDEN

Lou Cook
WEBSTER PARISH

Raisin Pie

SERVES 6-8

1 1/2 cups sugar
3 eggs
2/3 cup raisins
1/2 lb. butter or oleo
1 1/2 tsp. vanilla

Cover raisins with hot water and bring to a boil. Simmer until raisins are plump. Drain and cool. Add melted butter and vanilla to 1 1/4 cups sugar. Separate eggs and add beaten yolks to mixture. Use the remaining 1/4 cup sugar to beaten egg whites. Fold egg whites into mixture. Pour into unbaked pie shell. Bake at 350 degrees until top of pie is brown. Turn oven temperature down to 250 degrees. Bake 30 to 40 minutes longer.

MOORINGSPORT

Patsy (Bootsie) Lowe
CADDO PARISH

A Glass of Dessert

SERVES 8-9

6 large scoops vanilla ice cream
3 oz. Cream de Coco
7 oz. Brandy

Put all ingredients in a blender and mix well. Pour into champagne glasses.

MT. LEBANON

Mrs. Charles W. Eaton
BIENVILLE PARISH

Butternut Fruit Cake

SERVES 8-10

1 cup oleo, melted
1/2 cup white sugar
1 1/2 cups brown sugar
4 large eggs
1 cup pear preserves
1 1/2 tsp. butternut flavoring
1 cup Angle Flake coconut
1 1/2 cups pecans
2/3 cup raisins, brown or gold

2 cups self-rising flour
1 cup self-rising flour to
   dredge nuts and fruit
1 can Eagle Brand
   condensed milk
1 tsp. vanilla
1 cup candied cherries,
   cut in half
1 cup candied pineapple,
   chopped

Cream oleo, sugars and eggs. Add milk and flour, then
flavorings. Mix with mixer. Mix by hand the preserves and
coconut. Dredge nuts and fruit and raisins in the 1 cup of
flour and add to the batter. Place in greased pans and bake
about 1 hour at 325 degrees. I use a bundt pan and 2 small
loaf pans. Test for doneness. If you desire to decorate with
candied pineapple, put it on the bottom, then add batter.

NATCHEZ

Martha Lane
NATCHITOCHES PARISH

Aunt Virgie's Peach Cobbler
SERVES 8-10

Step 1
1 (29 oz.) can sliced
   peaches, in syrup
1 cup sugar
3 tbsp. flour
3 tbsp. butter or margarine
1 tsp. almond flavoring

Step 2
1 cup sugar
3/4 cup flour
2 tsp. baking powder
3/4 cup milk
1/4 tsp. salt, optional
3 tbsp. butter or margarine

STEP 1: Mix sugar and flour in medium saucepan. Add peaches with syrup and butter or margarine. Stir and cook over medium heat until fruit mixture comes to a boil. Continue cooking until mixture thickens. Add almond flavoring. STEP 2: Stir together in mixing bowl the sugar, flour, baking powder and salt, if desired. Add milk and mix well with wire whisk. Melt butter or margarine in baking dish (9" X 9" X 2" or slightly larger). Pour flour and sugar mixture in baking dish. Pour fruit mixture over the flour and sugar mixture. Bake 30 minutes at 350 degrees until golden brown on top. Serve in bowls while still warm. Even more delicious with a scoop of vanilla ice cream on top.

NATCHITOCHES

Sally Hunt
NATCHITOCHES PARISH

Rusty's Bread Pudding

SERVES 15

15-20 day old yeast rolls
3 cups sugar
5 eggs
1/2 gallon sweet milk,
   more or less
Vanilla and nutmeg to taste
1/2 lb. melted margarine
1 cup brown sugar, optional

SAUCE:
2 cups milk
1 cup sugar
Vanilla and nutmeg to taste
2 tbsp. flour
Rum, optional
Margarine

PUDDING: Crumble yeast rolls, add 3 cups sugar, and 5 eggs. Mix as you add the ingredients. Add vanilla, nutmeg and milk and mix well. Line pan with melted margarine, pour in pudding mixture and bake slowly in 300 degree oven approximately 1 hour.

SAUCE: Mix 2 cups milk with 1 cup sugar, bring to a slow boil, add vanilla and nutmeg. Mix 2 tbsp. flour with enough melted margarine to make a thick paste. Add this to the sugar and milk mixture, continuing to cook slowly until sauce thickens. Pour over bread pudding to serve.

OIL CITY

Rusty Batts/Rusty's Place
CADDO PARISH

Kake's Devil's Food Cake

SERVES 10-12

1 cup sugar
1 cup shortening
1/2 cup boiling water
2 squares unsweetened chocolate
1/2 cup buttermilk
1 tsp. vanilla
2 eggs, unbeaten
1 1/2 cups flour
1 tsp. baking powder
1 tsp. soda
1/2 tsp. salt

Cream shortening, then gradually add sugar. Cream thoroughly. Melt chocolate in 1/2 cup boiling water, let melt and mix well, then add to creamed sugar and shortening. After this is mixed well add eggs one at a time and beat well after each addition. Add vanilla to milk and add to cake mixture, alternating with sifted dry ingredients. Bake in two cake pans at about 350 degrees.

PLAIN DEALING

Ruby Kelly
BOSSIER PARISH

Granny Brown's Soft Molasses Cookies

SERVES 12

6 cups sifted plain flour	1/4 tsp. cloves
1 tsp. baking powder	1 cup shortening
1 tsp. salt	1 cup sugar
1 tbsp. soda	1 egg
1 tbsp. cinnamon	2 cups molasses
1 1/2 tsp. ginger	1 cup hot water

Measure and sift all dry ingredients. Cream shortening and sugar. Add flour mixture until blended. Add egg, molasses and hot water, beating well. Chill dough thoroughly and roll thin. (Try to determine how thick you want the cookie, it rises a good bit.) Cut in desired shapes and bake at 375 degrees on ungreased cookie sheet for 12-15 minutes or until done. Frost with thin sugar icing if desired, although they are delicious left plain. They are better if left closed in a tin for a few days.

PLEASANT HILL

Mickey Veuleman
SABINE PARISH

3 Flavor Pound Cake

SERVES 12

2 sticks oleo	1/2 tsp. baking powder
1/2 cup Crisco	1/2 tsp. salt
3 cups sugar	1 cup milk
5 eggs	GLAZE:
1 tsp. rum extract	1 cup sugar
1 tsp. coconut extract	1/2 cup water
3 cups flour	1 tsp. almond extract

Mix butter and Crisco. Add sugar slowly. Add eggs, one at a time. Add rum and coconut extract and mix well. Sift flour, baking powder and salt together. Add flour and milk alternately to cream mixture. Beat only enough to thoroughly mix ingredients. Bake 1 hour and 30 minutes at 325 degrees in a bundt pan. Glaze: Mix all ingredients and bring to a boil and boil about 2 minutes. Remove from heat and cool. Spoon over cake while it is still warm.

PROVENCAL

Mary Brister
NATCHITOCHES PARISH

Sylvia's Peanut Oatmeal Chewies

SERVES 20

1 1/2 cups brown sugar
1 cup peanut butter
3/4 cup margarine
1/3 cup water
1 egg
1 tsp. vanilla
3 cups oatmeal
3/4 cup raisins
1 1/2 cups plain flour
1/2 tsp. baking soda

Beat sugar, peanut butter and margarine until fluffy. Blend in water, eggs and vanilla. Add combined dry ingredients, mix well. Chill dough about 1 hour. Heat oven to 350 degrees. Form balls 1 1/2 inches. Flatten with bottom of glass. Place on an ungreased cookie sheet. Bake 12 to 14 minutes. If stored, cover tightly.

QUITMAN

Sylvia S. Comer
JACKSON PARISH

Lady Finger Cake

SERVES 8

2 packages lady fingers
1 pt. heavy cream
1 1/2 (8 oz.) packages cream cheese
1 tbsp. vanilla
1/2 cup sugar
1 can pie filling

Beat heavy cream until fluffy, about 10 minutes. Cream sugar and cream cheese together. Add vanilla. Mix in heavy cream. Cover bottom and sides of spring form pan with lady fingers. Spread half of cream mixture on lady fingers. Add layer of lady fingers, top with remaining cream mixture. Top with pie filling and chill for 2 to 3 hours.
* Twinkies can be substituted for lady fingers.

RINGGOLD

Pat Wilhite
BIENVILLE PARISH

Chiffon Pie

SERVES 8

1 1/2 cups crushed pineapple
1 (3 oz.) package Jello,
  (Any flavor, its just for color.)
3/4 cup sugar
1 cup undiluted Pet milk
1 tbsp. lemon juice
1 baked pie crust

Drain pineapple, add Jello and sugar. Cook until well dissolved. Place in refrigerator until stiff. Whip very stiff, Pet milk and lemon juice. (Pet milk has to be nearly frozen to whip.) Mix with pineapple mixture and pour into prepared pie crust and place in refrigerator until set. A very good Easter or Christmas dessert.

ROBELINE

Nell McQueen
NATCHITOCHES PARISH

Mama Jones' Tea Cakes

SERVES 12

1 cup sugar
2 eggs
2 tbsp. buttermilk
1 1/2 tsp. vanilla
2 1/2 cups flour
1/2 tsp. soda
1/2 tsp. baking powder
3/4 cup butter

Mix sugar, eggs, butter, buttermilk and vanilla. Sift together flour, soda and baking powder. Mix egg and flour mixtures. Stir and knead until smooth. If dough is too soft add more flour, or if too stiff add more milk. Roll dough on floured cloth or wax paper until 1/4 inch thick. Cut with floured cookie cutter. Bake at 375 degrees until golden.

ROCKY MOUNT

Rose Ann Holomon
BOSSIER PARISH

David's Blueberry Pie
SERVES 15

1 stick oleo, melted
2 cups graham cracker crumbs
1/2 cup powdered sugar
1/2 cup pecans, chopped
1 (8 oz.) package cream cheese
3 eggs
1 cup sugar
1 can blueberry pie filling
1 package Cool Whip

Mix graham cracker crumbs, oleo, sugar and pecans and spread in pie pan. Beat together cream cheese, eggs and sugar and spread over crust. Bake 20 minutes at 350 degrees. Cool. Spread blueberry pie filling over baked pie. Top with Cool Whip.

RODESSA

Billie Ruth Fletcher
CADDO PARISH

Cherry Cheesecake

SERVES 16-20

2 cups graham crackers,
  crushed
1/2 tsp. cinnamon
1/3 cup sugar
3 tbsp. melted butter
FILLING:
4 (8 oz.) containers
  cream cheese

4 large eggs, beaten
1/4 cup flour
1 tbsp. lemon juice
1 tbsp. vanilla
1 1/2 cups sugar
1/2 cup whipping cream
TOPPING:
1 can cherry pie filling

Mix crust ingredients and press into bottom of a 9" spring form pan. Soften cream cheese. Add beaten eggs, flour, lemon juice, vanilla and sugar. Blend together into a creamy mixture. Add whipping cream. Mix well. Pour into pan over crust. Bake at 350 degrees for 50 minutes. Turn off heat, leaving in oven with oven door ajar, to cool for 1 hour. Remove from oven and pan. Pour cherry pie filling over top. Serve.

RUSTON

Debbie Price
LINCOLN PARISH

Orange Pineapple Salad

SERVES 6

1/2 cup sugar
1 large can crushed pineapple
1 (16 oz.) box orange Jello
1 large container Cool Whip
1 cup grated cheese
1 cup nuts

Add sugar to pineapple and heat until boiling. Remove from heat. Add dry Jello and dissolve. Add 2 cups cold water and chill until it begins to congeal. Fold in Cool Whip, cheese and nuts and let jell.

SALINE

Janette Davis
BIENVILLE PARISH

"Lizzies"

SERVES 12

1 cup brown sugar
1/2 cup butter
4 eggs
1 scant tsp. soda
3 tbsp. milk
1 1/2 lbs. pecans, shelled
1 lb. candied cherries
3 cups sifted flour
1 tsp. cinnamon
1 tsp. all spice
1 tsp. nutmeg
1 cup whiskey

Mix soda and milk together. Add sugar, butter and eggs. Mix well. Add remaining ingredients and mix. Drop by teaspoonful on lightly greased cookie sheet. Bake at 300 degrees for 15-20 minutes.

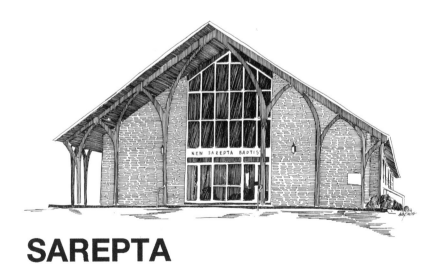

SAREPTA

Lori Hughes
WEBSTER PARISH

Mimi's Special Pie
SERVES 6-8

3 eggs
3/4 cup sugar
3 tbsp. margarine
1/8 tsp. salt
1/2 tsp. vanilla
1 cup Karo syrup
1 cup pecans
1/2 cup Angle Flake coconut
1/2 cup raisins

Beat eggs lightly. Add sugar and margarine. Add other
ingredients and pour mixture into an unbaked 10" pastry
shell. Bake in a slow 300 degree oven for one hour or until
set. Very good.

SHONGALOO

Evelyn M. Hines
WEBSTER PARISH

"Pinch Me" Cake

SERVES 10-12

2 cans biscuits
1/2 cup margarine or butter, melted
1 1/2 cups granola cereal
3/4 cup firmly packed brown sugar
1 1/2 tsp. cinnamon

Cut each biscuit in half. Dip each biscuit half into butter.
Roll in combined cereal, sugar and cinnamon. Layer in
greased 12 cup ring cake pan. Sprinkle with remaining
cereal mixture. Drizzle with remaining butter. Bake at 375
degrees for 25 to 30 minutes. Immediately turn onto serving
plate. Do not cut to serve, let people "pinch off" their own
piece.

SHREVEPORT

Georgia Davis
CADDO PARISH

Mary's Sweet Potato Pie
SERVES 6

4 medium sweet potatoes, peeled
3 cups sugar
2 sticks butter, softened
3 eggs
1 cup whole milk or 1 small can evaporated milk
4 tbsp. vanilla butternut flavoring

Boil sweet potatoes until tender. Drain off water and mash potatoes until all lumps are gone, with mixer. Add sugar, milk, butter, eggs and flavorings. Mix well. Pour mixture into pie shell and bake at 350 degrees for 40 to 45 minutes. This recipe makes two pies.

SIMSBORO

Mary Williams
LINCOLN PARISH

Mamaw Nelson's Rum Cake

SERVES 12

1 cup chopped pecans
1 box yellow cake mix
1 small package instant
  vanilla pudding
4 eggs
1/2 cup cold water
1/2 cup vegetable oil
1/2 cup light rum

GLAZE:
1/4 lb. margarine
1/4 cup water
1 cup sugar
1/2 cup light rum

Preheat oven to 325 degrees. Grease and flour a 10" tube pan. Sprinkle nuts on bottom of pan. Mix all other ingredients together. Pour over nuts. Bake for 1 hour. Cool. Invert on plate. Prick the top with a fork. Drizzle glaze over cake and allow glaze to absorb. GLAZE: Melt butter in pan. Stir in water and sugar. Boil for 5 minutes. Remove from heat. Stir in rum. Pour over cooled cake.

SPRINGHILL

Tracie Bryan
WEBSTER PARISH

Deb's Cornmeal Cookies

SERVES 6-8

3/4 cup sugar
3/4 cup butter or shortening
1 egg
1 1/2 cups flour
1/2 cup cornmeal
1 tsp. baking powder
1/4 tsp. salt
1 tsp. vanilla

Mix butter and sugar. Add egg. Mix well. Add rest of ingredients and mix well. Drop by teaspoon on greased cookie sheet. Bake at 350 degrees for 10 to 15 minutes or until a light golden brown. Makes about 2 dozen.

STANLEY

Deborah Wilkinson
DESOTO PARISH

Cow Patties

SERVES 12-15

1 cup Crisco
1 cup oleo
2 cups brown sugar
2 cups granulated sugar
4 eggs
1 tsp. vanilla
1 cup chopped pecans
4 cups flour
2 tsp. soda
2 tsp. baking powder
2 cups oatmeal
1 (6 oz.) package chocolate chips
1 (6 oz.) package butterscotch chips
2 cups crushed cornflakes

Cream Crisco, oleo and sugar. Add eggs and beat well. Gradually add and stir in the remaining ingredients. Drop by teaspoonfuls on ungreased cookie sheet. Bake at 325 degrees for 10 to 12 minutes. Makes several dozen.

SUMMERFIELD

Karla Aycock
CLAIBORNE PARISH

Garden Tea Room Bread Pudding

SERVES 24

1 loaf French bread, sliced, toasted, & crumbled
2 1/2 cups sugar
2 cups nuts
6 eggs
1 qt. milk
1 tbsp. cinnamon
1 tbsp. nutmeg
SAUCE:
1 box powdered sugar
1/2 cup evaporated milk
2 tbsp. rum

Toast and crumble bread a day ahead. Mix all ingredients
for pudding . Bake 45 minutes at 350 degrees in a 11 1/2"
X 15" baking pan. Mix sauce ingredients and spoon over
bread pudding. Heat pudding and sauce before serving.

VIVIAN

Garden Tea Room
CADDO PARISH

Gooey Cake

SERVES 8-12

1 box yellow cake mix
1 egg
1 stick softened butter
1 (8 oz.) softened cream cheese
2 eggs
1 box powdered sugar

Mix first three ingredients and pat into 13" X 9" pan. Mix next three ingredients and pour over first layer. Bake at 350 degrees for about 30 minutes. To make it slice well into squares, let cool for 2 to 3 hours.

WINNFIELD

Betty Turner
WINN PARISH

Granny Square Pie

SERVES 8-10

1 cup flour
1 stick butter
1 cup chopped nuts
1 (8 oz.) container cream cheese
1 cup powdered sugar
1 cup Cool Whip
2 boxes instant pudding
3 cups milk

Mix flour, butter and nuts and bake in a square pan at 350 degrees until golden brown. Mix cream cheese and powdered sugar until smooth. Fold in Cool Whip and spread over cooled crust. Mix pudding and milk and spread over cream cheese layer. Top with Cool Whip. Chill and enjoy.

ZWOLLE

Rhonda Cates
SABINE PARISH

269

THE BLANKS HOUSE, COLUMBIA, LA.

Northeast Section

Baskin
Bastrop
Bernice
Calhoun
Clarks
Clayton
Columbia
Crowville
Delhi
Epps
Farmerville
Ferriday
Forest
Gilbert
Grayson
Harrisonburg
Jena
Junction City
Kelly
Lake Providence
Lockhart
Mangham
Mer Rouge
Monroe
Newellton
Oak Grove
Oak Ridge
Pioneer
Rayville
Sicily Island
Spearsville

St. Joseph
Sterlington
Tallulah
Translyvania
Tullos
Urania
Vidalia
Waterproof
West Monroe
Winnsboro
Wisner

UNION
Bayou
D'Arbonne
MOREHOUSE
WEST CARROLL
EAST CARROLL
RICHLAND
Bayou Macon
OUACHITA
Ouachita River
MADISON
FRANKLIN
CALDWELL
TENSAS
Tensas River
CATAHOULA
LASALLE
MISSISSIPPI RIVER
CONCORDIA
Black River
MISSISSIPPI

White Cake

SERVES 10-12

2 1/2 cups sugar
1 cup Crisco shortening
4 cups flour
1 1/2 cups milk
4 tsp. baking powder
8 egg whites
1 tsp. almond extract

Sift flour once, measure 4 cups, add baking powder and sift 3 times. Cream shortening, add sugar gradually and cream together until light and fluffy. Add flour alternately with milk, a small amount at a time, beating after each addition until smooth. Add almond extract. Beat egg whites until stiff. Stir quickly into batter. Pour into 4 greased and floured 9" round pans. Bake in 375 degree oven for 20 to 25 minutes. Cover with desired filling.

BASKIN

Kathlyn Goforth
FRANKLIN PARISH

Chocolate Cookie Sheet Cake

SERVES 24

2 cups flour
2 cups sugar
1/2 tsp. salt
2 sticks margarine
1 cup water
3 tbsp. cocoa
2 eggs, beaten
1/2 cup buttermilk
1 tsp. soda

1 tsp. vanilla
FROSTING:
1 stick margarine
3 tbsp. cocoa
6 tbsp. milk
1 box powdered sugar
1 cup pecans, chopped
1 tsp. vanilla

Sift flour, measure, resift with sugar and salt. Put margarine, water and cocoa in saucepan. Bring to a boil and pour
over flour and sugar mixture. In another bowl mix eggs,
soda, buttermilk and vanilla. Add to chocolate mixture and
mix well. Bake in greased and floured shallow cake pan for
20 minutes at 350 degrees. ICING: Mix margarine, cocoa
and milk in saucepan. Heat on low but do not boil. Remove
from heat and add powdered sugar, pecans and vanilla.
Mix well. Frost cake as soon as it is removed from the oven.

BASTROP

Candy Nugent
MOREHOUSE PARISH

Vi's Pound Cake

SERVES 12

1 box Duncan Hines butter cake mix
1/2 cup sugar
5 eggs
2/3 cup Wesson Oil
1 tsp. vanilla flavoring
1/2 tsp. lemon flavoring
1/2 tsp. butter flavoring
1 (8 oz.) container sour cream

Blend and mix together sugar, eggs, oil and flavorings. Add cake mix and mix well. Then blend in sour cream. Bake in greased and floured tube pan at 350 degrees for 35 to 45 minutes until done. Ovens may vary; it is a good idea to check occasionally with a toothpick.

BERNICE

Vi Harlow
UNION PARISH

Apple Sauce Cake
SERVES 10

2 cups sugar
2 sticks oleo
3 cups flour
1/4 tsp. salt
1 tsp. soda
1/4 tsp. cloves
1/4 tsp. nutmeg
1/4 tsp. allspice
1/4 tsp. cinnamon
2 1/2 cups applesauce
1 tsp. vanilla
1 package raisins
3 cups nuts, chopped
1/2 lb. candied cherries, chopped
1/2 lb. candied pineapple, chopped

Cream sugar and oleo. Add applesauce and soda. Add the dry ingredients. Add fruit and nuts last. Bake at 325 degrees until done. Let cool in pan. No eggs in this recipe.

CALHOUN

Tom Hodge
OUACHITA PARISH

Yam Chiffon Tarts

SERVES 12

1 tbsp. gelatin
1/4 cup cold water
2 eggs, separated
1/2 cup maple syrup
1/2 tsp. cinnamon
1/2 tsp. mapleline
1/2 tsp. salt
1 cup strained Louisiana yams
1/2 cup rich milk
1/2 cup sugar
1/2 cup whipping cream
12 baked tart shells

Soak gelatin in cold water. Mix egg yolks, syrup, spices, salt and yams. Stir in milk and cook in double boiler until thick, stirring constantly. Remove from heat and add gelatin. Chill in ice water until mixture begins to congeal. Stir frequently. Beat egg whites until stiff, but not dry. Gradually beat sugar into whites until stiff and carefully fold into potato mixture. Fill tart shells. Serve, topped with whipped cream, chopped pecans and a cherry with a stem.

CLARKS

Pat Tarver
CALDWELL PARISH

Bobbye's Cherry Crunch

SERVES 12

2 cups plain flour, unsifted
2 sticks oleo, room temperature
2 cups chopped pecans or walnuts
1 box powdered sugar
1 (8 oz.) package cream cheese
1 (8 oz.) package Cool Whip
1 large can cherry pie filling

Mix with hands flour, oleo and pecans. Pat out on bottom of 9" X 13" casserole dish. Bake at 350 degrees for 20 minutes or until light brown. Put aside. Cream together powdered sugar, cream cheese and Cool Whip. Spread over first mixture when it is cooled. Top with cherry pie filling. It is best when it is refrigerated overnight.

CLAYTON

Mrs. Bobbye McIntosh
CONCORDIA PARISH

English Trifle

SERVES 20-24

18-20 slices pound cake
1 cup blackberry jam, strained
3 cups fresh blackberries
1 large package vanilla pudding
2 cups whipping cream, whipped
1/2 cup Cream Sherry
1/3 cup toasted, slivered almonds

Prepare vanilla pudding according to package directions.
Cool and fold 1/2 of the whipped cream into the pudding.
Pour 3 tbsp. of sherry into deep, clear serving dish. Turn
dish to coat dish well with sherry. Spread one side of cake
slice with strained jam and sprinkle other side with sherry.
Arrange cake slices around side of dish. Place 2 or 3 pieces
in bottom. Fill dish alternating pudding, berries and cake
slices. Top with remaining whipped cream. Sprinkle with
slivered almonds. Refrigerate.

COLUMBIA

Hazel Watts
CALDWELL PARISH

Juicy Coconut Cake

SERVES 12

2/3 cup soft shortening
1 1/2 cups sugar
3 eggs
2 1/2 cups all-purpose flour
2 1/2 tsp. baking powder
1 tsp. salt
1 cup milk
1 tsp. vanilla

ICING:
1 large fresh coconut,
    grated
1 3/4 cups milk from coconut
2 1/2 cups sugar
1 tsp. vanilla

Grease and flour 2 9" cake pans. Preheat oven to 350 degrees. Cream together shortening and sugar. Add eggs, beating thoroughly after each addition. Sift together flour, baking powder and salt. Add dry ingredients alternately with milk to creamed mixture. Add vanilla. Pour into prepared pans. Bake 25 to 30 minutes in preheated oven.
ICING: Put grated coconut and milk from coconut in saucepan. Add sugar and cook over medium heat about 15 to 18 minutes. Coconut will turn kind of clear. Add vanilla. Let set a minute or two and spread between layers and on top, making sure you use all the juice.

CROWVILLE

Julia Nelson
FRANKLIN PARISH

Punch Bowl Cake

SERVES 10

1 box yellow cake mix
1 container frozen strawberries
1 jar strawberry glaze
1 large box instant vanilla pudding
4 bananas
1 can blueberry pie filling
1 container of Cool Whip
Milk
Pecans

Bake the cake mix per instructions on the box, on a large cookie sheet. (Cake must be thin.) Let cool and cut in 1 inch squares. Prepare the vanilla instant pudding as directed on box. Set aside. Layer in a trifle bowl as follows:
Layer of cake. Layer of strawberries. Layer of glaze. Layer of Cool Whip. Layer of cake. Layer of blueberries. Layer of Cool Whip. Layer of cake. Layer of bananas. Layer of pudding mix. Layer of Cool Whip. Sprinkle pecans on top and CHILL OVERNIGHT........

DELHI

Glenda Cash
RICHLAND PARISH

Pol's Apple Cake

SERVES 10

3 eggs
1 1/4 cups oil
2 cups sugar
2 cups self-rising flour
2 medium apples, peeled, cored, chopped
1 cup shredded coconut
1 cup pecans, chopped
TOPPING:
1/2 stick butter
1/2 cup brown sugar
1/3 cup milk

Grease and flour a tube cake pan and preheat the oven to 350 degrees. Blend eggs, oil and sugar until creamy. Add flour a little at a time. Blend well. Batter will be stiff. Fold in apples, coconut and nuts. Pour into tube pan and bake for one hour. Cool for 30 minutes and remove from pan. Prepare topping: Mix butter, sugar and milk in a saucepan. Boil three minutes. Pour over cake.

EPPS

Denise Crane
WEST CARROLL PARISH

Sweet Potato Pudding
SERVES 6

1 lb. raw sweet potatoes
3/4 cup sugar
2 cups milk
3 eggs, well beaten
2 tbsp. butter
1 tsp. cinnamon
1/2 tsp. nutmeg
1/2 tsp. ginger
1/2 tsp. salt

Grate sweet potatoes and mix all ingredients together.
Bake in buttered baking dish 45 minutes at 350 degrees.
Apples, dates, pecans, pineapple or raisins may be added if
desired.

FARMERVILLE

Helen D. Owen
UNION PARISH

Mama's Blueberry Pound Cake

SERVES 12

3 cups sugar
2 sticks oleo
1 (8 oz.) package cream cheese
1 stick butter
1 tsp. vanilla
6 eggs
3 cups plain flour (cake flour best)
1 1/2 cups blueberries

Cream sugar, oleo, cream cheese and butter. Add eggs
one at a time then flour and vanilla. Blueberries may be
mixed with batter or fill pan half way with batter and add
blueberries, then cover with remaining batter. Start this in a
cold oven and bake 1 1/2 hours at 325 degrees. This cake
will stay moist for a long time.

FERRIDAY

Connie Seyfarth
CONCORDIA PARISH

Pineapple Upside Down Cake

SERVES 12

1 cup brown sugar
1 (15 oz.) can sliced pineapple
1 stick butter
Cherries
1 cup regular sugar
3 eggs, separated
1 cup flour
5 tbsp. pineapple juice
1 tsp. vanilla

Put brown sugar and butter in large skillet and melt. Spread evenly. Place pineapple rings in skillet and place a cherry in the center of each pineapple ring. Cream sugar and egg yolks. Add pineapple juice and flour, alternately. Beat egg whites and fold into cake mixture. Add vanilla and mix well. Pour over pineapple in skillet. Bake at 350 degrees for 45 minutes.

FOREST

Louise Gunter
WEST CARROLL PARISH

Ola's Blackberry Pie

SERVES 6-8

4 cups blackberries
1/3 cup water
1 cup sugar
2 tbsp. flour
Butter

In a saucepan, toss berries, sugar and flour. Add water, put lid on saucepan and place over low heat until berries are wilted and juice has thickened. While berries are cooking make a pie crust and roll to 1/8" thickness. Using a 10" square pan or Pyrex dish cut a piece of crust large enough to cover the bottom and come up the sides (about 11" square) of the pan. Place the dough in the dish or pan. Cut another piece of dough 10" square and set aside. Cut the remainder of the dough in strips and bake on a cookie sheet at 400 degrees. When berries are ready, cover the bottom of the uncooked crust with 1 cup berries. Place a layer of cooked strips on the berries. Cover this with berries. Continue alternating cooked strips and berries. Place the uncooked 10" square on top of last berries. Dot with butter and bake at 400 degrees until brown. Serve with Cool Whip or whipped cream.

GILBERT

Margaret Dosher
FRANKLIN PARISH

Angel Food Parfait

SERVES 10-12

1 small angel food cake
1 large box strawberry Jello
3 cups chopped fresh strawberries
   or 2 boxes frozen strawberries, drained
1 pt. whipping cream, whipped

Tear angel food cake into bite size pieces. Prepare Jello according to package directions, add strawberries and place in refrigerator to thicken slightly. Fold cream into angel food pieces, then fold in congealed strawberries. Pile into parfait dishes and top with whipped cream and one strawberry to garnish. NOTE: Substitute sugar free Jello and Cool Whip for a lower calorie dessert.

GRAYSON

Karen Cruse
CALDWELL PARISH

$100.00 Devil's Food Cake

SERVES 15

1 cup mayonnaise
1 cup sugar
1 (9 oz.) bottle Maraschino
cherries, chopped
1 cup liquid, cherry juice
and water
2 cups cake flour
3 tbsp. cocoa
2 tsp. soda
Vanilla

ICING:
3 cups powdered sugar
3 tbsp. cocoa
1 stick butter
1 (4 oz.) cream cheese
1 tsp. vanilla
1/8 tsp. almond flavoring

In large mixing bowl, mix all ingredients, blending well with mixer. Pour batter into two 9" cake pans, lined with wax paper, and sprayed well. Place in cool oven and bake 30 minutes at 350 degrees. If necessary reduce heat near the end of the baking time. When done, turn layers onto a cake rack. Let cool before removing. Handle these layers with caution. ICING: Cream ingredients well, using mixer. If necessary a little cream may be added to the icing.

HARRISONBURG

Lucille Taliaferro
CATAHOULA PARISH

A "Nutter" Cheesecake

SERVES 10

2 (8 oz.) packages cream cheese
1 1/2 cups sugar
6 eggs
1/2 tsp. vanilla extract
1 box "Nutter Butter Bites"
1 (16 oz.) carton sour cream

Mix sugar into softened cream cheese. Add vanilla extract.
Add well beaten eggs to mixture. Fold in box of Nutter
Butter Bites. Bake in greased spring pan in pre-heated 350
degree oven for 25 minutes. Cut off oven and open oven
door; leave cake in oven (with door open) for 45 minutes.
Remove cake, spread sour cream on top and chill several
hours.

JENA

Bobbie Dean
LASALLE PARISH

Hot Fudge Pudding Cake

SERVES 12

1 cup all-purpose flour
3/4 cup granulated sugar
2 tbsp. cocoa
2 tsp. baking powder
1/4 tsp. salt
1/2 cup milk
2 tbsp. shortening, melted
1 cup chopped nuts
1 cup brown sugar
1/2 cup cocoa
1 3/4 cups hot water

Mix flour, sugar, 2 tbsp. cocoa, baking powder and salt in mixing bowl. Blend in milk and shortening. Stir in nuts. Pour in ungreased square pan. Stir together brown sugar and 1/2 cup cocoa and sprinkle over batter. Pour hot water over batter. Bake 45 minutes in preheated 350 degree oven. Eat while still warm.

JUNCTION CITY

Gail Sehon
UNION PARISH

Chocolate Fudge

SERVES 15 to 20

5 cups sugar
1 large can evaporated milk
5 tbsp. cocoa, rounded
2 tbsp. white Karo
2 sticks margarine
2 tbsp. vanilla

Mix first four ingredients in a heavy boiler. Bring to a rolling boil. Lower heat to a steady boil. Boil until mixture forms a soft ball that can be worked by hand. Turn off heat. Add 2 sticks margarine and 2 tbsp. vanilla. Beat about 5 minutes. Let rest about 10 minutes. Beat another 5 minutes. Let rest another 10 minutes. Now beat until mixture looses it's gloss and begins to get real firm.. Pour into buttered dish with sides large enough to hold fudge mixture. When cool cut into squares. Pack in airtight container.

KELLY

Floyce Childress
CALDWELL PARISH

Mother's Best Chocolate Pie

SERVES 10

1 cup sugar
3 tbsp. flour
3 tbsp. cocoa
2 cups milk
1 tsp. vanilla
3 eggs
1 9" baked pie shell

Sift flour, sugar and cocoa together. Whip egg yolks until light and add to milk. Place milk and eggs on stove to heat, then add flour, sugar and cocoa. Stir constantly and cook until thick and smooth. Add vanilla and pour into baked pie shell. Top with meringue made by folding 3 tbsp. of sugar into beaten egg whites.

LAKE PROVIDENCE

Eloise F. McKenzie
EAST CARROLL PARISH

Easy Lemon Pie

SERVES 6-8

1 can Eagle Brand milk
1 egg
1 package unsweetened (yellow) lemonade-Kool-Aid
1 graham cracker pie crust

Mix first three ingredients together and pour into crust. Chill and Serve.

LOCKHART

Patricia S. Loyd
UNION PARISH

Boeuf River Ice Cream

SERVES 20-25

9 eggs, medium sized
1/2 gallon milk
2 1/2 cups sugar
Dash of salt
1 tbsp. vanilla
1 (12 oz.) can cold evaporated milk, whipped

Beat eggs until well blended. Add milk, sugar and salt.
Cook over low heat or in double boiler over water, stirring
constantly until mixture begins to thicken and coats a
spoon. Remove from heat and cool completely. Add vanilla
and whipped evaporated milk and stir until mixed. Pour into
a five or six quart freezer. (Variations: 1-banana- add 1/2
sugar to 3 mashed ripe bananas plus a dash more of salt.
Add to cooled custard. 2-strawberry- add 1/2 cup sugar to
1 pint thoroughly mashed strawberries. Add to cooled
custard.)

MANGHAM

Barbara M. Boies
RICHLAND PARISH

Nana's Banana Pie

SERVES 4-6

3-4 bananas
1 cup sugar
2 heaping tbsp. flour
1 cup milk
4 eggs, separated
2 tbsp. butter
1 tsp. vanilla
1 baked pie crust

Mix sugar, flour, milk and egg yolks in order listed. Cook over low heat or in double boiler until thick. Add butter and vanilla. Cool and pour over sliced bananas which have been placed in cooled pie crust. Top with meringue which has been made with reserved egg whites. Bake in 325 degree oven until light golden brown.

MER ROUGE

Wallace McLendon
MOREHOUSE PARISH

Coconut Pecan Delight

SERVES 12

1 1/2 cups unsifted all-purpose flour
1 cup chopped pecans
1/2 cup melted butter or margarine
2 2/3 cups flaked coconut
1 (8 oz.) package cream cheese, softened
3 cups cold milk
1 package vanilla instant pudding, (6 serving size)
1 (8 oz.) container whipped topping

Combine flour, 1/2 cup pecans and the butter, mix until flour
is moistened. Press evenly into 13" X 9" pan. Bake at 350
degrees for 15 minutes. Cool. Toast remaining pecans and
2/3 cup of coconut on baking sheet at 325 degrees for
about 5 minutes until lightly brown. Beat cream cheese until
very soft. Gradually add 1/2 cup milk and blend until
smooth. Add remaining milk and the pudding mix. Beat on
low speed until well blended, about 2 minutes. Stir in remaining coconut and pour immediately over baked crust.
Spread whipped topping evenly over pudding. Sprinkle with
toasted coconut and pecans. Chill at least 2 hours. Cut
into rectangles.

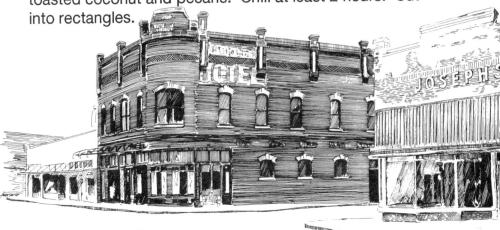

MONROE

Marilyn Baer
OUACHITA PARISH

Pineapple Pie

SERVES 6-8

1 can condensed milk
1/2 cup lemon juice
1 (20 oz.) can crushed pineapple, drained
1 (8 oz.) container Cool Whip
1 graham cracker crust

Combine condensed milk and lemon juice. Stir well. Fold in crushed pineapple and Cool Whip. Pour into graham cracker crust. Chill.

NEWELLTON

Pauline Patton
TENSAS PARISH

Three Day Coconut Cake

SERVES 20

1 Yellow Pillsbury Plus cake mix
1 1/2 cups sugar
1 (12 oz.) container coconut
1 (12 oz.) box cool whip
1/2 can cream of coconut
1 (8 oz.) container sour cream

Cook cake mix according to directions on box. Bake in three layers-(Cool). Mix 1 1/2 cups sugar, 8 oz. sour cream and 3/4 of the coconut plus one cup Cool Whip. When cake is cool spread bottom layer with cream of coconut, then spread a thick layer of sugar, coconut, sour cream mixture on top of that. Spread in same order on second layer. (There should be 1 cup of filling left so add 2 cups of Cool Whip to it and spread on top and sides of cake. Sprinkle rest of package of coconut on top and store in Tupperware cake carrier for 3 days in the refrigerator. This makes a very moist cake.

OAK GROVE

Elna Brasher
WEST CARROLL PARISH

Baked Egg Custard

SERVES 6-8

2 cups dry bread crumbs
4 cups milk, scalded
2 tbsp. butter or oleo
1/4 tsp. salt
1 tsp. vanilla
1 cup sugar
4 eggs, slightly beaten
   (It is better to use 8 egg yolks)

Soak bread crumbs in scalded hot milk for 5 minutes. Add butter, salt and sugar and mix well. Pour slowly over eggs. Add vanilla and mix well. Pour into greased baking dish. Bake in a pan of hot water in a 325 degree oven until firm, about 1 hour.

OAK RIDGE

Marion Files
MOREHOUSE PARISH

Sweet Potato Pie

SERVES 8

1 9" unbaked pie shell
2 cups cooked sweet potatoes, mashed
1/2 cup butter or margarine, softened
2 eggs, separated
1 cup firmly packed brown sugar
1/4 tsp. salt
1/2 tsp. cinnamon
1/2 tsp. ground nutmeg
1/2 tsp. ground ginger
1/2 cup milk
1/4 cup sugar

Combine sweet potatoes, butter, egg yolks, brown sugar, salt and spices. Stir in milk and mix well. Beat egg whites at high speed of electric mixer for 1 minute. Gradually add 1/4 cup sugar, 1 tbsp. at a time, beating until stiff peaks form. Fold egg whites into sweet potato mixture. Spoon mixture into unbaked pie shell. Bake at 400 degrees for 10 minutes. Reduce heat to 350 degrees and bake for 45 minutes longer or until set.

PIONEER

Pat Copes
WEST CARROLL PARISH

Rocke Road Peanut Butter Squares

SERVES 12-16

3/4 cup light corn syrup
1/2 cup sugar
3/4 cup peanut butter
6 cups Rice Krispies
2 cups miniature marshmallows
1/2 cup chopped nuts
1/2 cup chocolate chips
1 tbsp. shortening

Heat corn syrup and sugar to boiling, remove from heat and add peanut butter and stir until melted. Place cereal in large bowl. Pour boiled mixture over cereal and stir until cereal is coated. Cool 2 minutes and stir in marshmallows. Pour into a 13" X 9" X 2" pan. Sprinkle with nuts. Melt chocolate chips and shortening together and pour over top. Cut into squares.

RAYVILLE

Dottie Harrington
RICHLAND PARISH

Oreo Delight

SERVES 8-10

1ST LAYER:
1 (16 oz.) package Oreos
1 1/2 sticks margarine
2ND LAYER:
1/2 large Cool Whip
2 cups powdered sugar
1 (8 oz.) package
  cream cheese

3RD LAYER:
1 cup pecans, chopped
4TH LAYER:
1 (5.9 oz.) box instant
  chocolate pudding
5TH LAYER:
1/2 large Cool Whip

Crush Oreos (save 1 cup for topping). Melt margarine, pour over Oreos. Press in bottom of pan. Cream together 2nd layer and spread over Oreo layer. Sprinkle pecans over 2nd layer. Prepare pudding according to package directions. Pour chocolate pudding over pecans. Spread 1/2 large Cool Whip over chocolate pudding. Sprinkle remaining Oreos for topping.

SICILY ISLAND

Mrs. Raymond Peace
CATAHOULA PARISH

Peaches and Cream

SERVES 8

3/4 cup flour
3/4 cup milk
1 egg
1 large can sliced peaches
1 large box vanilla instant pudding
2 tbsp. butter
1 (8 oz.) package cream cheese
3/4 cup sugar

Mix flour, milk, juice from 1 can peaches and vanilla pudding. Melt butter in 9" X 13" X 2" pan. Pour above mixture over the butter. Arrange peaches on top of mixture. Mix cream cheese, softened with sugar. Spoon over peaches. Bake in 350 degree oven until brown around edges. Middle will be runny but will get firm as it cools.

SPEARSVILLE

Kathy Bryan
UNION PARISH

"Lite" Chocolate Pie

SERVES 6

2 tbsp. cocoa	2 1/2 cups skimmed milk, scalded
2 tbsp. diet butter	3 eggs, separated
1/3 cup flour	3/4 tsp. vanilla
1 cup sugar	1/3 cup sugar
1/4 tsp. salt	8" pie shell, baked

Melt chocolate and butter over hot water in the top of a double boiler. Mix flour, sugar and salt and stir into chocolate. Add milk slowly and stir constantly until mixture is fully thickened, about 15 minutes. Beat egg yolks well. Stir in a little of the chocolate mixture, then pour into rest of hot mixture and cook 2 minutes, stirring constantly. Remove from heat, cool partially and stir in vanilla. Pour into pie shell. Beat egg whites until stiff, then slowly beat in the 1/3 cup sugar until stiff. Swirl meringue over pie and cook in 350 degree oven 12 to 15 minutes or until brown.

ST. JOSEPH

Jo Ann McDaniel
TENSAS PARISH

Angel Pie

SERVES 8

CRUST:
4 egg whites
1/4 tsp. cream of tartar
1 cup sugar
FILLING:
4 egg yolks
3/4 cup sugar

1/2 cup flour
2 cups milk
2 tsp. sherry extract
1 tsp. vanilla
1 1/2 squares bitter chocolate
2 tbsp. butter
Whipped cream

CRUST: Beat egg whites until frothy. Add cream of tartar and continue to beat until it holds a stiff peak. Gradually beat in sugar. Beat until it looks glossy like divinity. Spread in greased pie plate. Bake at 250 to 300 degrees for 1 hour and 10 minutes. Allow to cool. Remove about a 4 to 5 inch circle on top of the crust.

FILLING: Beat egg yolks. Scald milk and melt chocolate in double boiler. Add yolks. Mix sugar and flour and gradually mix in liquid. Cook until thick. Add butter and extract. Pour filling in crust and top with whip cream. Put topping that was removed from crust over top of whip cream. Refrigerate 4 hours before serving.

STERLINGTON

Lorraine Gregg
OUACHITA PARISH

German Chocolate Angel Food Refrigerator Cake

SERVES 8-10

4 cakes German
   sweet chocolate, (1 lb.)
8 tbsp. boiling water
6 eggs, separated
1 tsp. vanilla

1 box Duncan Hines
   angel food cake,
   bake as directed
1 pt. whipping cream,
   whipped and sweetened

In double boiler melt chocolate with water. Cool slightly. Beat egg yolks and add chocolate, vanilla and stiffly beaten egg whites. Pour over Angle Food cake which has been broken into 1 in. pieces. Pack into 9 in., waxed paper lined spring form pan. Refrigerate several hours. Remove rim and turn out as you would a cake. Remove wax paper and ice with sweetened whipped cream.

TALLULAH

Bobbe H. Cox
MADISON PARISH

Banana Blueberry Cream Pie

SERVES 8

2 9" pie shells, baked
2 envelopes Dream Whip
1 1/2 cups sugar
1 can blueberry pie filling
2 large bananas, sliced
4 (3 oz.) packages cream cheese
Juice of 1 lemon

Line pie crust with bananas.
Prepare Dream Whip as directed
on package. Combine cream
cheese, sugar and lemon juice.
Fold in Dream Whip and spread
over bananas. Top with the
blueberry pie filling. Refrigerate.

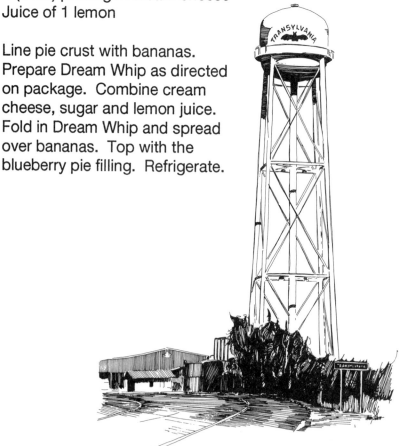

TRANSYLVANIA

Cheryl Winstead
E.AST CARROLL PARISH

The Greatest Pecan Pie

SERVES 6-8

1 cup sugar
1 cup white Karo syrup
3 eggs
1/2 tsp. salt
1 tsp. butter, melted
3 tbsp. corn meal
1 tsp. vanilla
1 1/2 cups pecans

Beat eggs well and set aside. Add all the other ingredients except pecans. Add the eggs and mix well. Finally add the pecans to the mixture. Pour into a 9" unbaked pie shell. Bake at 400 degrees for 10 minutes. Reduce heat to 300 degrees and bake for an hour. This pie has an unusual taste. It's not too sweet but just sweet enough. I know you will love it.

TULLOS

Mavis Richardel
LASALLE PARISH

Angel's Delight

SERVES 16-20

1 (10") Angel Food Cake, bought or homemade
1 small package vanilla pudding
1 (8 oz.) package of cream cheese
1 cup sugar, divided
1 can condensed milk
1 (12 oz.) Cool Whip, divided
1 quart strawberries, fresh or frozen

Crumble Angel Food Cake. Put half the crumbs in a large bowl. Slice strawberries, add 1/2 cup sugar and set aside. Mix pudding according to box directions and set aside. Mix cream cheese and the other 1/2 cup of sugar. Add pudding to cheese mixture. Fold in condensed milk and then 1 1/2 cups Cool Whip. Add half of the the strawberries to crumbled cake and then add half the pudding mixture. Repeat layers of cake, strawberries and pudding. Cover with the rest of Cool Whip. Decorate with more strawberries.

URANIA

Nola Fae Wilson
LASALLE PARISH

Pina Colada Cake

SERVES 10-15

1 box yellow cake mix
1 can condensed milk
1 (12 oz.) bowl Cool Whip
1 can cream of coconut
1 can coconut
1/2 cup chopped pecans

Make cake as directed on box. Pour into 9" X 13" pan and bake. Mix cream of coconut and condensed milk. When cake has baked, punch holes in cake with fork. Sprinkle 1/2 of coconut on cake and pour milk mixture over coconut. Mix pecans and Cool Whip and spread over cake. Sprinkle with remaining coconut and refrigerate. A coconut lovers dream.

VIDALIA

Carolyn F. Smith/Smith Printing
CONCORDIA PARISH

Orange Pecans

SERVES 10

1 cup sugar
4 tbsp. margarine
3 1/2 cups pecan halves
1/4 cup frozen orange juice concentrate, undiluted
1 tsp. vanilla

Mix sugar, orange juice and margarine and bring to a boil in a 4 quart boiler. Boil 1/2 minute only. Add vanilla, stir well and add pecan halves. Beat until mixture thickens slightly. Pour on waxed paper. Let cool and separate. Great for party nibblers.

WATERPROOF

Beverly M. Rushing
TENSAS PARISH

Banana Caramel Pie

SERVES 8

4 medium bananas
2 cans Eagle Brand sweetened condensed milk
Whipping cream
Graham crackers
1/2 stick butter
1 tbsp. milk
1/2 tsp. vanilla
1 tsp. sugar

Crush graham crackers until fine crumbs. Add butter and milk and blend well. Press on bottom of a pie pan and up the sides about 1 inch. Slice bananas. Use about two bananas to make first layer. Using a double boiler, heat condensed milk over high heat for 1-1/2 hours or until thick and caramel colored. Remove from heat. Stir and pour 1/2 of the caramel over the banana layer. Slice 2 bananas to make second layer. Pour remaining caramel over banana layer. Beat whipping cream until stiff, add sugar and vanilla if desired. Spread over top of pie.

WEST MONROE

Jackie Dunn and Diane Humble
OUACHITA PARISH

Pineapple Sorbet

SERVES 10-12

2 cups sugar
2 cups water
4 cups pureed pineapple
10 pureed cherries

Make a simple syrup by boiling sugar and water together until sugar is dissolved. Add pineapple and cherries and freeze in ice cream freezer.

WINNSBORO

Peggy Ellington
FRANKLIN PARISH

Earthquake Cake

SERVES 12

1 cup coconut
1 cup pecans, chopped
1 box Swiss chocolate cake mix
1 (8 oz.) package cream cheese, room temperature
1 stick butter, softened
1 (1 lb.) box powdered sugar

Grease and flour the bottom of a 9" X 12" pan. Mix coconut and pecans together and put in bottom of baking pan. Mix cake mix according to package directions. Pour over pecans and coconut. Mix the cream cheese, butter and powdered sugar together until creamy. Drop by spoonfuls over the top of the cake batter. Bake at 350 degrees for 30 to 35 minutes or until cake is done. Refrigerate cake after it has thoroughly cooled.

WISNER

Elsie B. LeMoine
FRANKLIN PARISH

Town Index

Town Index

Town Index

Town Index

Recipe Index

Recipe Index

Recipe Index

Recipe Index

Please send_____copies of the Louisiana Proud Collection of Sweet Things at $12.95 per copy. (Postage for 1 book is $1.75. Add $.25 for each additional copy.)

NAME_____

ADDRESS_____

CITY_____STATE_____ZIP_____

___Please send a Louisiana Proud Product Brochure

LOUISIANA PROUD
6133 Goodwood Ave. Baton Rouge, Louisiana 70806

• •

Please send_____copies of the Louisiana Proud Collection of Sweet Things at $12.95 per copy. (Postage for 1 book is $1.75. Add $.25 for each additional copy.)

NAME_____

ADDRESS_____

CITY_____STATE_____ZIP_____

___Please send a Louisiana Proud Product Brochure

LOUISIANA PROUD
6133 Goodwood Ave. Baton Rouge, Louisiana 70806